Serving
as
SENDERS
Today

Serving as Senders—Today is formatted for individual and group study. Each of the eight study sessions has sections dealing with:

- For Your Personal Involvement
- Action Steps
- Group Discussion
- For Further Action

Serving as Senders—Today is also available as a six-hour live or DVD seminar (www.eri.org).

TWENTIETH ANNIVERSARY EDITION
Revised & Expanded

Serving
as
SENDERS
Today

Neal Pirolo

Also by Neal Pirolo:
Serving as Senders
The Reentry Team
I Think God Wants Me to be a Missionary
By Neal & Yvonne Pirolo:
Prepare For Battle

First printing, March 2012
Second printing, April 2013

ISBN 978-1-880185-24-7

Some Scripture quotations are paraphrases by the author.

The opening story in Chapter Five is adapted from *In Other Words*, October 1990 issue, and is used by permission from Wycliffe Bible Translators. The second story in Chapter Five is from *Mission Catalyst*, and is used with permission. In many stories the names and locations have been changed to protect the innocent (and the guilty).

16 printings of *Serving As Senders* in American English
Over 400,000 copies in print, in 20 languages

Published by Emmaus Road International, Inc.
7150 Tanner Court, San Diego, California 92111

Printed in the United States of America

To the many
cross-cultural workers
and their support teams
out of whose experiences
come the pages of this book.

Acknowledgments

"Now unto Him who is able to do exceeding abundantly above all that we can ask or think; unto Him be glory throughout all ages."
Ephesians 3:20

I N *Serving as Senders*, we wrote, "Who would have thought that the birthing of such a little book would require such labor? Yet, who would have thought of the joy it also would bring? The coaching team was great!" We had no idea that from a modest print run of 3000 would come over 400,000 copies in 20 languages!

We continue to acknowledge our dependence on God, the Holy Spirit, Who is our inspiration and Divine Teacher.

My wife, Yvonne, has been a total support through the years of writing and rewriting each new print run. And now again, with forthright critique she has added her personality to this edition.

We acknowledge Julie Brown, our Administrative Assistant, who used up the red ink of her favorite pen to add her thoughts and grammatical corrections.

Also, to the many whose life stories have made this a *Today* edition.

And we would still acknowledge the friends of El Adobe Trust who funded the first printing, for without that, we would not be here today!

Contents

Preface

I SAT IN THE UPPER level of the auditorium at the University of Illinois in Urbana, listening to the heavyweights of the evangelical community challenge 17,000 college students to a vital and personal commitment to world evangelization. It was InterVarsity's Urbana Student Missions Conference.

I must admit I had begun daydreaming when all of a sudden there was the statement: "In secular war, for every one person on the front line of battle, there are nine others backing him up in what is called the 'line of communication.'"

The concept exploded in my mind like a mortar shell! The speaker had been drawing a parallel between secular war and the spiritual warfare that accompanies cross-cultural ministry. He continued, "And how can we expect to win with any less than that ratio? God is not looking for Lone Rangers or Superstars; He is commanding an army—soldiers of the Cross."

I said, "Thank You, Lord, for that confirmation!" At that time I was directing a one-year ministry school, which had a strong emphasis on cross-cultural outreach. Though I had no background in secular war, as soon as students applied to the school, I had been encouraging them to build around themselves a team of *nine* people who would support them in prayer, since enrolling in this school was saying to the enemy, "I am getting out of the pew and onto the battlefield!"

Since that evening at Urbana, with more vigor than ever, I have encouraged, exhorted—even implored—anyone going into cross-cultural outreach ministry to not leave home without a strong, committed support team—a group that accepts the ministry of serving as senders.

In 1983, I was being encouraged to seek new direction in ministry. My counselor-friends believed (among other things) that the ministry would encircle the globe (not in my wildest dreams!). However, by God's grace it has happened. With *Serving As Senders* now in 20 languages, the book and its principles of member care have ignited and fueled a worldwide awareness of and action to *"the most hurting link in today's mission movement."* (Quote by the late Dr. Ralph Winter.)

It has been an awesome privilege to continue to promote the cause of member care. Whether with a denomination in Spain or a national missions conference in Guatemala; whether with a young church sending out its first missionary through a Saturday seminar or a movement of churches at their annual conference, my heart continues to beat to the rhythm of better care for cross-cultural workers.

Through the years, some clarity has come to me, to understand that there are four levels of member care:

- Agency Level
- Church Level
- Personal/Relational Level
- Crisis Level

Each level of care functions better at one point or another. And, as the first three fulfill their function in cooperation and harmony, there is a lesser need for the fourth level. Unfortunately, though, in every battle there are bound to be some casualties.

The principles of this volume touch primarily on the third level: Personal/Relational Care. The goal is for the missionary to develop a partnership team who share the same vision with him, who have an equal commitment to their God-given task, who focus their energy on that area of care, and who will share the joy of victory through Jesus Christ. For, after all, it is Jesus Christ who will build His Church (Matthew 16:18).

By the time you're through with your study of this book, you'll be able to answer this question: "How can I get involved in the Great Commission of world evangelization even though I know I am called to stay at home?" You can become personally involved in the mission process as a sender.

Ministering by His grace,
Neal Pirolo
San Diego, California

~~~ • ~~~

**Because of the impact of many of the original stories,
they have been retained in this revised edition.
Many new stories further illustrate
the need for senders.**

CHAPTER 1

The Need For Senders

"And how shall they [go] preach except they are sent?"
Romans 10:15

"**B**ETH! WAKE UP! Please, Beth! Wake up!" Beth's roommate held the empty Valium bottle in her hand and knew Beth wouldn't wake up. But instinct said to get help. The people in the next apartment helped her carry Beth to the car. A mile that seemed half way around the world brought them to the hospital. They pumped Beth's stomach. She stirred and opened her eyes.

Months later Beth could talk about it:

"I had had a normal life before this. Friends, a loving family, a good church life. Basically, I was a happy person. I had been a professional for ten years. I had held reputable positions. I had managed people. And I had managed myself quite well ... until this.

"I had just returned from a six-month missionary venture in Asia. My feelings were running rampant. Nostalgia flooded me as I remembered the good times; nightmares and flashbacks haunted me in the quiet solitude of night. Nobody was interested; nobody had time to hear what I had to say.

"I had just come from a fruitful experience as an administrative assistant in a medical clinic. Dumped back into the busy lifestyle of metropolitan Washington, D.C., I lost all sense of identity. Deepening feelings of isolation caused me to withdraw all the more.

"I thought if I got back into my work I could refocus my life. But the emotional instability mounted. One nightmare kept recurring:

"We had been in a village doing some medical work. Through the thundering of a tropical storm, I awoke to the sound of gunfire. Before I could go back to sleep, I saw them dragging the body of a man past the doorway of my hut. The story was that he had been caught in the fields stealing opium.

"Now back in D.C., I would awaken at night to the sounds in my brain of the pow-pow of the guns. And the whole ugly scene would flash through my mind again. I began using tranquilizers to control my instability. But before seven or eight in the evening, I was lost in anxiety, confusion, uncertainty— crying uncontrollably.

"Conversely, I also had a sense of 'special' knowledge. I was fulfilled by a good missionary experience. Hadn't I been there? Hadn't I been successful? Hadn't I bonded with and nurtured Billy to health?

"We had been on our way home from some medical work in the hill country. Along the trail I stumbled on this three-month-old infant. His hands and feet were bound together with rope. He was addicted to opium. He was almost dead. We inquired as best we could whose son he was. The man who was thought to be the father was away on 'business' three to four weeks at a time. His mother already had four children under the age of five.

"It was probably this woman who had left him there to die. A couple hundred yards away was an abandoned hut. We said we would wait there until nighttime to talk with his mother. She never came. At the clinic we were able to give him the care needed. We called him Billy. A local Christian doctor eventually adopted him.

"I became hyper-vigilant about the great needs throughout the world. I felt a lot of anger toward people who wouldn't let me talk about my experiences. My pastor wouldn't let me share at church. No Sunday school class had the time for me. My parents couldn't show enough interest to even look at my pictures. I became judgmental and condemning: 'How can you be thinking about buying a new car when there are such great needs out there?' But I couldn't say any of that out loud. Hurt, fear, anger and guilt all turned inward in severe depression. I couldn't sleep at night; I couldn't get out of bed in the morning. I quit my job. I took more and more tranquilizers. I just wanted somebody to acknowledge that I was back home!

"One Sunday morning after church, I gathered the strength to again go to my pastor and say, 'I am at the end of my rope! I think I'm losing it! I need your help!' With his arm around me, he said, 'Beth, I am busy. I am so tied up this week. But if you must, call my office to set an appointment for a week from Wednesday. Beth, if you would just get into the Word more. ...'

"Through the dazed fog of the existence I had been living in, all of a sudden it became crystal clear: 'Pastor, I'm not worth your time!' I had made other desperate calls to various counselors. One tried to date me. A psychiatrist had given my condition a fancy label. But now it was clear: 'I'm not worth anybody's time!'

"I decided to swallow the rest of the Valium pills."

It would astound most Christians to hear missionaries honestly express their desperate need for support in one area or another. Most pleas aren't as dramatic as Beth's. Yet, too many cries for help do end in death. Each appeal speaks of a personal need to those who will come alongside them and serve as senders.

Missions should not just focus on those who go. Those who serve as senders are equally significant.

A BIBLICAL FOUNDATION

If anybody knew about going on missionary journeys and needing a support team, it was the Apostle Paul. He said, "... and how can they [go] preach except they are sent?" In Romans Chapter Ten, he established the vitality of cross-cultural outreach on these two levels of involvement: *Those who go and those who serve as senders.*

Paul first quoted Joel: "For whosoever shall call upon the name of the Lord shall be saved." Then, in clear, gapless linear logic so well understood by the Roman mind, he appealed: "How then shall they call on Him in whom they have not believed? And how shall they believe in Him of whom they have not heard?"

Today's estimate is that about half of the earth's population still has not heard a culturally relevant presentation of the Gospel.

"And how shall they hear without a *preacher*?" Yes, there must be a "preacher"—the missionary, the cross-cultural worker, the *one who goes.* By whatever name and by whatever means he gets there, there must be a proclaimer of the Good News. God chose it to be this way. (Throughout our study, we'll be referring to your missionary with a generic "he"—though at times we could mean *he, she* or *they*!)

> "And how shall they preach except they are *sent?*"

Though the total missions force is decreasing from Western nations, God is sovereignly raising up an army of workers from Southern and Eastern countries. But the cry of our Lord two thousand years ago still rings true: "The harvest is plentiful; the laborers are few" (Matthew 9:37). And unfortunately, because of this, this is where most mission conferences end their appeal. "We need more missionaries," comes their cry.

But wait. There is one more question in this series: "And how shall they preach unless they are *sent*?" (Romans 10:13-15). Paul acknowledged that there are others besides those who go who must be involved in this worldwide evangelization endeavor: Those who are serving as senders.

Those who go and those who serve as senders merge their callings and talents and giftings to form the cross-cultural outreach team. All are equally important. All are vitally involved in the fulfillment of the Great Commission. All are dynamically integrated and moving toward the same goal. And all are assured success, for those in God's work are on the winning team!

From the humble beginnings of one hundred young people at the Mount Hermon Meeting of 1886, during the next five decades, the Student Volunteer Movement identified and fielded over 20,000 men and women to be goers—set apart to declare the Gospel and teachings of Christ to a lost world.

This same movement mobilized an army in excess of 80,000 mission-minded people who pledged themselves to stay at home and support those who went.

In the year 2000, 40 small congregations in Brasilia, Brazil joined together to send their first missionary team. Eleven years later, as the Church in Brazil has taken a lead role in missionary sending, church after church is responding to the call for "the rest of the team"—those who will serve as senders.

In decades past, many grew up in mission-minded churches. Men and women from faraway places came to speak of the challenge to follow in their steps. It was easy for the listener to understand the importance of those who go. But they were also left with the feeling that if they were not called to go, the only alternative was to give them some money, wish them well and say, "Goodbye!"

This whole scenario, of course, was punctuated with the story of David's men who were too tired to go on, but they would receive an equal share in the spoils. (Read I Samuel 30, but *don't* use it to "encourage" your support teams!) To those who are already feeling that they are "second class" because they are not "giving up everything and going," this story only emphasizes their feelings of not being good enough. Paul's words in Romans 10 (considered above) lay the correct foundation: The effectiveness of those who go is contingent on those who serve as senders.

There are some people in your fellowship—I'm sure of it— who want to be involved in world evangelization but don't feel called to go right now. By you reading this book, I would say *you* might be one of them! The good news is there's more that you can do than just say "goodbye!"

There is a tremendous need for senders. And the need goes far beyond the traditional token involvement of showing up for a farewell party or writing out a check to missions. A cross-cultural worker needs the support of a team of people while he is preparing to go, while he is on the field and when he returns home.

A careful reading of Paul's missionary letters will reveal how much time he spent talking to his support team—those who were involved with him in the ministry. Sometimes he complimented them, sometimes he expressed his loneliness in being away from them, and some times he exhorted and challenged them. But he always thanked God for them.

A support team of senders is just as critical to a missionary today. Let's look at some very good reasons why.

A CROSS-CULTURAL WORKER'S LIFE TIME-LINE

Consider this diagram of the physical/emotional/mental/ spiritual life time-line of a cross-cultural worker during his missionary experience.

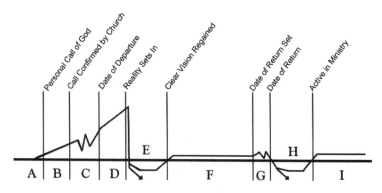

**Cross-Cultural Worker's
Life Time-Line**

A. "Normal" Living

The flat, horizontal line of this diagram represents the "normal living" base line of your missionary's life before he even had a thought about missions. This is *not* to say that his life (or yours) was flat! There were normal ups and downs, but for the purpose of comparison, consider the line as his *normal* life before he began thinking about cross-cultural ministry.

The line that resembles the dips and curves is the changing pulse of your missionary friend's entire being as he passes through his cross-cultural experience. It is important to note that the progression through these segments of time is not just for long-term commitments. Even a ministry trip of three weeks can experience some very interesting ups and downs. Members of short ministry trips also need a sending team.

The vertical lines indicate segments of time, signposts along his missionary venture. The relative spaces between the lines may vary due to many factors. But these are expected phases of which you, his support person, should be aware. As you are giving your support, anticipate the next signpost of your cross-cultural worker's life time-line, and be available to offer your assistance.

B. Anticipation of Approval

At some point, your missionary emerged from his closet of prayer, having grappled with all the normal feelings of inadequacy. Want to know how he probably felt? Read through Exodus Chapters Three and Four to hear the patriarch Moses rehearse his five excuses of inadequacy. "Who? Me? I'm not good enough to go!" was his first excuse. While you're reading, notice that God answered each of Moses' protests with His all-sufficiency. Boldly or with some reluctance, your friend announced that he believed God had placed a personal call on his life to become a missionary. Every fiber of his being has undergone a rise in excitement and apprehension, visions of grandeur and nightmares of depression.

Because one gentleman had been very active in his church

before he sensed a call to a longer-term commitment, it only took a brief time for the leadership to say, "Yes, we believe God wants us to send you." On the other hand, a woman who was offered a low-paying teaching job in a restricted country (a legal way to enter) was told by her leadership: "You are not going as a missionary. You are going to have a job, so we cannot send you." I trust your policies will embrace the former example, rather than the latter.

C. Pre-field Preparation

The church, mission board or other responsible body has confirmed that personal call with their approval (Acts 13:1-4). It has been determined that your friend is really going! No! There may be days, weeks, even months or years of preparation, support-team building and training. Anticipation continues to heighten as the date of departure draws near.

One gentleman contacted me, wanting his family to attend our pre-field training course before going to Hong Kong. I asked if his church leadership had prayed and laid hands on them as in Acts 13. His answer: "They don't know a thing about missions. They said for us to 'just go'!" I suggested that he should commit some time to building an awareness of missions and how to be a good sending church. He did, and when they went two years later, their time on the field benefited. After many years of cross-cultural ministry, he returned to that church as Missions Pastor.

D. Honeymoon Period

Your missionary is catapulted into the heavens in a jumbo jet, but his emotions are soaring high above that plane! The "honeymoon" has begun. For a period of time he moves around in a protective bubble, enjoying all of the quaint newness of his ministry environment. Even the single control on the shower that produces only cold water is "interesting." There is so much to observe, to take in. It's all so ... different! And wonderful!

Don't be surprised, however. Some honeymoon periods can be quite short. One seasoned missionary admitted her "honeymoon" lasted less than twenty-four hours. She arrived on the field to discover several tragic things that had happened in her absence. Her high hopes of quick accomplishment were delayed.

E. Culture Stress

It is important to remember that the time that passes between these identified stages will vary according to circumstances, and from family member to family member, as well as from missionary experience to missionary experience. But as surely as night follows day, this next stage is inevitable.

One morning your missionary rudely awakens to the reality that the single handle will never produce hot water! He realizes he has committed himself to circumstances that are no longer quaint; they are now weird, even barbaric! The adventure of discovery has turned to the dread of "What's next?" The first bugs of dysentery keep him up all night. The fact that this is the most difficult language in the world to learn has him looking for a permanent interpreter. The first hints of persecution or the awareness that people are not going to change as easily or as rapidly as he had hoped have him asking God: "Why are You doing this to me?" The pinnacles of ecstasy have plummeted to the depths of despair. Culture stress has set in. "What am I doing here?" he screams in silence.

Most missionaries don't want to talk about this stage of missionary life because the people back home won't think of them as "spiritual" enough if they admit to some of these trying times. It is at this time that your cross-cultural worker needs your support. Many—too many—crash here. Of course, some have been known to turn back before they leave the airport! Others, tragically, remain on the field, being able to offer nothing and draining the energy of others who are trying to buoy them up.

A missionary, already two years on the field, acknowledged that he was still very anxious, fearful and apprehensive—still experiencing the stress of living and ministering in a second culture.

F. Ministry of Love

But your missionary has been taught that culture stress is a normal stage. As Paul encouraged Timothy (1 and 2 Timothy), you are there to support your missionary friend through this time of disappointment. Therefore, he will do just that: Go through it into a beautiful time of ministry motivated by the love of Christ. Because of your strong support he will emerge with a strengthened vision

"Do you love us? Or are you just here to get a job done?"

of God's purposes in his life and his reasons for being a missionary. All is not rosy. The adversaries are there—but the "great, effectual open doors" of ministry that Paul talked about are there, too (1 Corinthians 16:9).

To complete a survey asked for by the director of an agency, one missionary was asking the nationals, "What do we look like to you? How can we be more culturally sensitive?" One woman, after two and a half hours of coaxing said, "Okay! Okay! Do you *really* want to know? *Do you love us? Or are you just here to get a job done?*" It was not necessary to ask her which of those she believed! A job *does* need to get done, but if it is motivated by love, that will show clearly.

G. Anticipation of Return

Life goes on. As surely as this missionary journey had a starting point, the time will come when your cross-cultural worker will, like Paul and Barnabas, "sail back to Antioch from where they had been recommended by the grace of God for the work which they had now completed" (Acts 14:26).

Again, his feelings are mixed. Yes, your missionary wants to come home to see you. But he has made new friends. He has new ideas and ideals. His heart has been moved with compassion for the lost; there are so few to take his place in ministry. The desire to stay and continue in ministry usually outweighs the desire to return home.

He has changed behavior patterns that he knows will be

difficult to integrate into his new home environment. No, he isn't returning to his old home environment when he comes back. For you also have changed! However, these changes in him and you have happened so gradually in their respective environments that neither he nor you think you have changed *that* much. Then, when you see each other: "Wow! Have you ever changed!" Thus, the physical/emotional/psychological/spiritual pulse of your missionary drops again.

Another devastating factor is that most missionaries do not take the time to do what is necessary during this period: Begin thinking about the changes he will face upon reentry. Instead, they work harder and longer to get just that one more thing done before leaving the field.

Unless you are there to remind him that Grandma died two years ago. Or that his favorite restaurant is now a freeway interchange. Or that the new pastor does not have the same heart for missions. Or …!

Probably the shortest letter ever written was to a missionary whose furlough time had been scheduled; all plans had been set. Then, remembering the difficulties of previous times back in the States, he wrote that he had changed his mind; he was not coming. The reply was sent back: "Pete! Get home!" He came and his support team was able to help him through the next stage.

H. Culture Stress in Reverse

In Chapter Seven, we deal extensively with the support your cross-cultural worker needs after his return. The trauma to his entire being during reentry is intense. An example is the reentry desperation of Beth whose story is told at the beginning of this chapter. In this great time of need, your missionary might feel especially inadequate to do anything about it.

During this time of reverse culture stress, coming back home mandates strong support. More missionaries are "lost" when they come home than when they go to the field! And many people just echo the words of an agency member care director when told the story of Beth. He said, "Oh, that sort of thing doesn't happen." However, a woman in his agency just three months prior to that statement had succeeded in committing suicide! Unfortunately, this time in the life of a missionary is still the least understood and given the least attention by the agency, the missionary or the people back home. Unless you are there for him!

(We have devoted an entire book to helping you learn how to care for your returning friend. *The Reentry Team: Caring for Your Returning Missionaries* is available at www.eri.org.)

I. Full Integration

A missionary who has been trained to anticipate the stress of coming home and has a strong reentry support team will, in time, fully integrate his changed self into the changed home environment. He will be a positive change-agent in his church and community. He will "abide a long time with the disciples there" (Acts 14:28). He will, like Paul, "continue in Antioch, teaching and preaching the Word" (Acts 15:35). And who knows? After a while he might even say, "Hey, Barnabas, let's go out again!" (Acts 15:36).

Today no cross-cultural worker should leave home without a strong, integrated, educated, knowledgeable, excited-as-he-is, active team of people who have committed themselves to the work of serving as senders.

You may be a part of that team. Your heart is stirred by people of other cultures, yet you have not heard His call to go. When a missionary speaks at your church, when you attend a Perspectives Course or you read of a tremendous breakthrough in some far off country, there is a special quickening in your pulse. Yet you know God has directed you to stay at home. You may be called to the ministry of serving as a sender.

Prayerfully consider serving as a sender in any one or more of six areas of care:

Moral Support—giving an encouraging word
Logistics Support—details, details, details

Financial Support—money, money, money
Prayer Support—intense spiritual warfare
Communication Support—emails, Skype, CDs, DVDs,
    visits and more
Reentry Support—helping him fully integrate his *new* self
    into his *new* environment

Each area has its unique responsibilities; each is best served by specific gifts within the Body of Christ. For example, if you have the gift of encouragement, it will be easier for you to give moral and communication support. The gift of administration will be very helpful for logistics support. To contribute to the financial support of your friend will be easier if you have the gift of giving. Vital to prayer support is the gift of intercession. Reentry support is greatly helped by those who exercise the gift of hospitality. Allow God's Spirit to speak to your heart about your possible involvement in any one or more of these areas of support.

God's *call* on your life to serve as a sender must be just as vibrant as the call on the life of the one you send. Likewise, the *commitment* you make must be as sure as that of your cross-cultural worker. The responsible *action* you take is as important as the ministry your field worker performs.

And the *reward* of souls for His Kingdom will be equal to your missionary's, as long as you are faithful to the task He has given you to do.

IT HAPPENED THIS WAY IN SAN DIEGO

I'm Not 'Gonna' Read 'Dat' Book! Steps to Partnership Development

"I'm not 'gonna' read 'dat' book! I've got the Bible and that's all I need," Byron yelled at his Missions Pastor. Byron had been on several short-term ventures. But on this most recent one, God had touched his heart with the need for a longer-term commitment. He had shared his vision (personal call) with his leadership (Acts 13:1). After some prayer and fasting (Acts 13:2), they sensed that God wanted them to send him to the mission field. The first step in preparation was to develop a partnership team. Byron wasn't prepared for that. Thus, his objection.

Dan, the missions pastor, gently but firmly informed Byron that without building a partnership team, the church would not be able to lay hands on him and send him out (Acts 13:3). Grudgingly, Byron began reading *Serving As Senders*.

Early into the book, he realized that this was important stuff. He began talking with his friends, telling them about what God was calling him to do and that he had come to realize that he couldn't do it on his own. He needed to develop a team of people who would join him in this ministry. He shared his vision with any and all who would listen. Even one time when he was standing in line at the grocery store, he began talking with the person behind him. A word of encouragement was given. At another store, a woman gave him some money! He had not asked for it, but she probably thought (as is too often the case) that that is all he wanted. Rather, he was just excited about what the Lord was allowing him to do—to build a team of warriors to support him even while he was preparing to go.

Well, he began having once a month meetings on Sunday afternoon. "No, you are not making a commitment yet," he would tell them. "Just come and hear what the Lord is doing and how you could be involved. Then you can prayerfully and intelligently make a decision." At each meeting he would share the excitement and anticipation he sensed in the teamwork that was developing. News from the field helped all to understand the significance of this ministry—that it was a decisive point of battle. (A decisive point of battle is one in which the objective is worth doing and there are sufficient resources to do it.)

He realized that the key person to find would be the team leader. "Out of sight, out of mind" is too strong a malady to expect that he could keep the team functioning from his place in Asia. Fortunately, a woman who had been a Bible school classmate sensed and caught Byron's enthusiasm for his appointed ministry. Knowing that God wanted her to stay home, yet greatly desiring to engage in the Great Commission, she prayed about this position of leadership. And God said, "Yes, Silvia, this is where I want you to minister!"

At meetings and through regularly talking with people, always exuding an excitement about the "team" concept of this venture of faith, Byron found the key leaders for the six areas of care that he knew he would need. He was learning how important a team would be to his success on the field, and to the strength he was beginning to feel in the solid support that was already building.

Anne had been a "spiritual mother" to him for many years. And Byron knew she was a prayer warrior. Would she be his prayer support leader? Again, after fully understanding the commitment she was making, and in prayer, she accepted this position.

Felix seemed to be a solid, business-like sort of guy. "Would he handle the financial support team?" Byron wondered.

David was a perfect fit for networking all of the logistical needs. And he jumped right in, long before Byron went to the field. So many details.

Being in a sensitive country, Byron knew that his communication support leader would have a big responsibility. All emails would be screened by him before they were sent on to Byron. Team meetings—yes, the team meetings continue monthly—would be his responsibility to announce. Byron's encrypted newsletter would be unscrambled by Lupe and forwarded to the team. He would be the lifeline link between Byron and the team.

Rather than selecting a specific person to head up the reentry support team, it was decided that the whole team, keeping in contact with him throughout his time on the field, would act as his reentry team. They later discovered this was a mistake; they needed a specific person to coordinate this time in Byron's life. (A task left to *everyone* is usually not handled by *anyone!*)

Also, (and correctly) they came to realize that the moral support—his need for encouragement—was coming through the very active role each was playing in their various responsibilities. His morale was high as this team continued to form. No specific person was needed to be a "cheerleader."

The team was set. All six areas of care were accounted for. Forms were handed out at each meeting. "Go home and pray about what God would want you to do," Byron would encourage. Each leader was notified as Byron received commitments from those he continued to talk with. He simply directed them to the team leader after they had prayed about what area of service the Lord had shown them to fulfill.

The meetings continued monthly. Others caught the vision and the excitement of being an active part of this mission. Not just an "I'll give you some money, and, oh, yes, I guess I can pray for you" type of involvement. But each one was sensing an ownership of this mission. "It is *our* mission," each one came to understand as they heard from the Lord about their part in it.

Once just a group of people, these servants of God realized they were being formed into a team! They were practicing together in giving Byron the moral support he needed as this or that detail didn't seem to be falling into place. At each meeting there was a time of prayer, not only for Byron, but also for the ministry to which he was going. In fact, as they saw it, they were *all* going with him, in spirit, though not in person.

Well, Byron went. The team continued to meet monthly. Others were added to the team as they found out about this opportunity to serve. About a year later, one Sunday afternoon, photos that Lupe had printed out from an email attachment were being passed around. A person sitting near the end of the circle exclaimed at one particular picture, "What is *this*?" That allowed the others who had already seen the picture to shout their questions! You see, "this" was a picture of Byron with a young lady's head on his shoulder!

"Who is this lady?" "Why didn't we know about this?" And other questions exploded in the room. "I am going to send him an email and let him know that we need to approve of this." Others echoed this sentiment, not realizing that all of their emails would end up in Lupe's IN box and have to be screened by him.

But the statement that rang loud and clear was the one by Anne, the prayer coordinator: "I want to know if this young lady is distracting Byron from doing what *we* sent him there to do!" You talk about ownership! This *team* was expressing that this is *our* mission. Byron is representing *us* in Asia. *Our* involvement is at stake here. *We* don't want anything to mess it up.

And in Silvia fashion, she took control of the situation. "Listen up! We know Byron. We know he is a godly man. We know that he has a passion for the ministry he is in. We know he would not do anything that would discredit our Lord's Name. We have

> "I want to know if this young lady is distracting him from what *we* sent him there to do!"

been praying for him. And let's pray now." And they did.

The saga continues. Does the team need a "shot in the arm" now and then? Certainly. Anything positive needs some external force countering the natural decay of non-attention.

What about the young lady? They were married with the blessings of their church leadership, the agency, their families and their support team. And I am sure, most of all; the blessings of God are on their lives together.

(In addition to the following individual study, see the Group Leader's Guide for Chapter One beginning on page 197.)

For Your Personal Involvement

Note: A text without a context is a pretext. Throughout this study you will find many Scripture references. To benefit more fully from the lessons, read each one in its full context. Allow the Holy Spirit to "guide you into all Truth" (John 16:13).

❑ Read Romans 10:13-15. From that passage, fill in the blanks in the following statements. Notice that there is a key word in each question that leads you to the next question. The foundation of the whole sequence, then, lies in the final word! Write that final word in all capital letters to highlight in your mind the vitality of serving as senders! However, remember that serving as senders is not *more* important than, but it is as important as, those who go (John 13:16b).

10:13   For whosoever shall _c all_ upon the Name of the Lord shall be SAVED (Joel 2:32).

10:14   How then shall they _call_ on Him in Whom they have not _believed_? And how shall they _believe_ in Him of Whom they have not _heard_? And how shall they _hear_ without a _preacher_?

10:15a   And how shall they _preach_ except they are _sent_?

10:15b   To bring the process full circle, Paul again quotes Scripture, "How beautiful are the feet of those who preach the Gospel of peace." Both those who go and those who serve as senders are equally needed for the missions process to be successful.

❑ List the nine stages of the physical/emotional/psychological/ spiritual life time-line of a missionary, and the incident in time that forms the transition from one to the next. (Note the example.)

Period A: _"Normal Living"_ ; _personal call_

Period B: _____ ; _____

Period C: _____ ; _____

Period D: _____ ; _____

Period E: _____ ; _____

Period F: _ministry of love_ ; _sme accultivation, prayer_

Period G: _anticipation of return_ ; _____

Period H: _____ ; _active in ministry_

Period I: _full re-integration_

❑ Read the following passages relating to Paul's need for a support team. Place in each blank the type of support Paul was either asking for or expressing thanks for— whether moral, logistics, financial, prayer, communication or reentry. Following the semicolon, place the gifting that would make serving in this area easier. (Each area is referred to in at least one passage.)

- Ephesians 6:18-19 _____; _____

- 2 Timothy 4:13 _____; _____

- Acts 14:26-28 _reentry_ ; _____

- Acts 21:12-13 _____; _____ ? moral

- Romans 16 _communication_ ; _____

- Philippians 4:10-12 _____; _____

❑ Reread Byron's story. Take special note of three things:
- How he developed his core team leadership; _monthly reg lar but not freq very_
- The vitality of the whole team in that "crisis" moment; _positive_
  and
- The *ownership* the team felt when *their* ministry was "threatened".

❑ Rank from 1-4 (with 1 as most important) how you think "cultural Christianity" estimate the value of the following people:
       _2_ Pastor   _1_ Missionary
       _4_ Layperson   _3_ Evangelist

Did you give the layperson the number 4? Now read 1 Corinthians 1:11-13; 3:4-9; 12:12-27 and Revelation 2:6,15. The doctrine of the Nicolaitans made a distinction between the clergy (professional religious people) and the laity (common, ordinary folk).

After prayer, fill in the following sentence:

I, _____**, as a sender,**
                    (your name)

am as important in God's global plan (but not more

important) as_____**, even**
                    (name a famous missionary)

though my role won't seem as dramatic.

Maybe you can't fill that in right now. Go ahead and read through *Serving As Senders—Today*. By the end of your study, we trust you will be able to make that statement personal! (Did you look up and read John 13:16b?)

ACTION STEPS

By the time you have read Chapter One, completed the *For Your Personal Involvement* section and participated in a group discussion, you should ...

- Sense the need for those who serve as senders.

- Want to study further to know where you might fit.

- Take the initiative. Let your missionary friend know that you are learning about the ministry of serving as a sender. And you will soon be available to help support him in one or more areas for God's glory! (Caution: It is possible that some others before you have made great promises of care for your friend, and have not followed through. Thus, your friend may be a bit hesitant to welcome your offer to help.)

- Multiply yourself. Look among your fellowship for those who seem to be at loose ends. Possibly they are the cross-cultural parts of your church. Invite them to read and study this book with you.

CHAPTER 2

Moral Support

*"Be strong and very courageous; don't be
afraid or dismayed: for the Lord your God
is with you wherever you go."*
Joshua 1:9

"IT WAS A BIT UNUSUAL. The rapid sequence of events,
that is. We raised up others to assume the ministries
we were doing in the church, got married, attended a
12-week field training course in Tijuana, Mexico, and spent our
first year together living on a kibbutz in Israel!

"But why not? We were young, adventurous and had not
yet accumulated a lot of the world's possessions. And most of
all, the church where we had been ministering for the past three
years was totally supportive. It was a small fellowship in a small
town, so everyone knew us. The smiles and hugs on Sunday
morning said to us, 'Scott and Jean, this is right!' Deep in our
own hearts, God's peace said, 'This is right!'

"Invitations to our wedding included a note requesting, 'No
gifts, please; we are going to Israel!' 'This is right!' they said
with their donations of money instead. A prayer of blessing by
our pastor at the wedding said, 'This is right!' Even our non-
Christian parents said, 'This is right!' The moral support from
every quarter said, 'This is right!'

"We began our training in Tijuana. We met our Mexican host

family. Classes began. Learning how to relate to each other—we had been married just four weeks—was the subject of one of the classes. We did our fieldwork in the community, grappling with cultural adaptation and relating to our host family with our limited Spanish. But with their patience and a lot of humor, we learned how to learn a second language and we bonded with them. Principles of spiritual warfare were preparing us for battle. We were learning how to live and minister in a second culture. Communication from our home church assured us that the sense of God's direction was solid. 'This is right,' we said to each other.

"Then, as a part of our training to make sure the support system was 'up and running,' we were sent home for a long weekend. We sat in the pastor's living room. Somehow there was an awkward feeling. We glanced at each other: 'This is not right!' we thought.

"Then Pastor Joe spoke: 'Scott and Jean, I have made the decision that you are not to continue in this mission!'

"We were stunned!

"Our objections were not too well thought out and they probably didn't make much sense since we were so confused. My wife started crying. Pastor Joe said firmly, 'Jean, I am not moved by your tears!' We were speechless! We became angry but he remained firm: 'You are not to go! If you continue, you are on your own!'

"We were dazed. The bottom had just fallen out! The very foundation of our support team was shattered! There was an empty feeling in the pit of our stomachs. We could hardly go to church. We weren't allowed to contact any of the people there for further support. 'This is not right!' we knew.

"Fortunately, a part of our support team was made up of individuals from several other churches and Bible study groups. As we all beseeched the Lord for His direction in this new situation, we came to believe that it wasn't that we shouldn't go, but that we were losing a vital part of our support team.

"Just before leaving for Israel, by chance we met Pastor Joe downtown. He was so convinced that God had spoken to him that he said if we continued on this venture, something bad was going to happen to us in Israel. He would stake his ministry on it!

"Needless to say, this added insult to injury. Not only had we lost a strong foundation of moral support, but also now this prediction was to cause a continual cloud of apprehension during our whole time. When anything risky or unknown loomed ahead, we would remember his statement. For example, one night at the kibbutz, a loud siren awakened us. We were ready to run for the bomb shelter as we had often practiced. 'This is it! What bad thing is going to happen to us?' we thought. But since we saw no one else running and the siren stopped, we went back to bed.

"The next day we discovered that the temperature in the turkey house had fallen below a safe level. This siren was to alert the men responsible to adjust the thermostat! Though the humor of that situation mellowed our apprehension, Pastor Joe's 'cloud of doom' hovered above every crisis.

"We returned home. It was a successful time of ministry in Israel. We found that God began healing our relationships with the people of that church. Pastor Joe did not quit his ministry—in fact, he agreed for us to share in one of the local outreaches of his church!"

Moral support is the very foundation of the support system. Everyone in the church can be involved in this part of the ministry since in its most basic concept, moral support is simply saying, "God bless you! We are excited with you in your missionary venture!"

The missionary also senses this level of support when those committed to the other areas of care are functioning well. Possibly the actions are appreciated even more than just words alone. Yet, a word fitly spoken—how good it is (Proverbs 25:11)!

Did the great men of the Bible need moral support? Let's look at a few of them.

BUT DAVID ENCOURAGED HIMSELF IN THE LORD

Jesse's other seven sons had been rejected. "For the Lord sees not as man sees; for man looks on the outward appearance, but the Lord looks on the heart." There yet remained one—a boy. A teenager. They brought him in from the fields where he was tending the sheep. And the Lord said, "Arise, anoint him, for this is he." And the Spirit of the Lord was on David from that day forward (1 Samuel 16).

Through the battle with Goliath, through the struggle with Saul's insane jealousy, through the war of nerves during the months and years of fleeing and being pursued by a king who was troubled by an evil spirit, through the conflict involved in building his royal entourage of six hundred ruthless men, the Spirit of the Lord was upon David (1 Samuel 17-29).

And as the Philistines were assembled against Israel, David and his men were with them. But a distrust of these Hebrews troubled the minds of the Philistine generals. David and his men were sent back to Ziklag—only to discover that the Amalekites had invaded from the south, burned the city and carried away all their wives and children. "And they wept, until they had no more power to weep. And David was deeply distressed, for the people spoke of stoning him. But David encouraged himself in the Lord" (1 Samuel 30).

Imagine the intensity of the moment—the physical distress of a three-day return march to Ziklag. The adrenaline rush that had built up for a battle against Israel and then the letdown. The bombarding emotions of losing family and possessions. The internal battle of "Lord, I am your anointed King of Israel. When am I going to possess the throne?" Where was David's moral support team? They wanted to stone him!

But David encouraged himself in the Lord.

My Hour Has Now Come

Eleven hundred years later. Another Man, another occasion. He says to His three-man support team, "My hour has come! My soul is exceedingly sorrowful and very heavy. Watch and pray with Me." And now the God-man, the Propitiation for our sins, the Lamb slain from before the foundations of the earth enters the most significant battle of all time.

The battle of wills rages. All of His humanness rises to say,

"Father, there must be another way. I cannot drink this cup of separation. We have been eternally One. Isn't there another way to redeem man back to You? Let this cup pass from Me!"

The anguish becomes intense, for He knows there is no other way. The mental and spiritual suffering of the incarnate God in atonement for the sins of fallen man leads Him to the extreme of physical torture: hematidrosis, the bloody sweat.

"Could you not watch with Me one hour?" Jesus questioned His followers. A second, and then a third time He came to them: "My hour has now come" (Matthew 26:36-45)!

In each of these situations there were those who could have been supportive. But David's men, so overcome by their own loss of wives and children and homes, thought only to stone David. Christ's men, self-indulgent in sleep, were not even aware of their Master's passion that night.

What of others? When Mary told Joseph she was pregnant by the Holy Spirit, his first response was to put her away privately (Matthew 1:19). In John 9, Jesus compassionately healed a blind man. When the Jewish elders wanted the parents' testimony in support of their son's healing, in fear of the Jewish leaders, they said, "Ask him! He's old enough to tell you!" When Paul was determined to go to Jerusalem, "we made every attempt to dissuade him," even though Agabus' prophetic statement did not say for him not to go (Acts 21:12-13).

The pages of history do not paint a brighter picture. Through the centuries, the pattern has not changed. Read about the bold men and women God told to go to the nations in Ruth Tucker's biographical history of Christian missions, *From Jerusalem to Irian Jaya*. You can count on the fingers of one hand the few who found strong moral support for their pioneer vision.

An English cobbler named William Carey struggled in the 1790s with the Church's responsibility to the Great Commission. Later he was to become known as the "Father of Modern Missions." But in his early days as the vision stirred deep in his heart, there was no support. His fellow churchmen openly rebuked him by saying, "When God pleases to convert the heathen, He will do it without your aid or ours." His wife initially refused to join him on his voyage to India. Only a delay in the departure date gave her the opportunity to reconsider.

Today as thousands of cross-cultural workers emerge from their closets of prayer, having grappled with the issues of being His soldiers of the cross in another culture, what sort of moral support can they anticipate from people?

- People so lost in their narrow world that they do not support God's anointed but rather begin hurling stones of incrimination—like David's men?

- People lulled into self-indulgent sleep to the extent that they are unaware of God's plan for their friends—like Jesus' disciples?

- People so concerned about public opinion that they want to nod nicely at missionary zeal but try to send their worker away privately—like Joseph?

- People so afraid for the other programs of their church that they don't want anything to do with daring adventures into the unknown, the uncomfortable? Mission ministry, after all, could be regarded as competition to the status quo—like the Jewish leaders asking about the blind man's healing.

- People who misunderstand a "word from the Lord" so that they disagree with the missionary's "hearing from the Lord"—like Paul's friends in Caesarea?

- People who pierce God's missionary heart by distorting their theology—like William Carey's friends?

ATTITUDES AND ACTIONS THAT DO NOT SUPPORT

Stones of incrimination. There are few who can handle the personal challenge presented to them by a friend who thinks God wants him to do such a bold, daring thing as go to the mission field. Whether ignorantly, out of well-meaning friendship or to assuage their own feelings of distress, they may begin hurling verbal attacks: "Man, it's a rough world out there! Riots and wars! Hatred and violence! Famine and disease!" (By the way, those should be reasons enough to go!)

Other callous responses might be: "I'm shocked! You? A missionary? What do you think anyone can do to save the world?" Another thought quickly follows: "You could get yourself killed!"

Often close, loving friends counsel:

- You're needed here. You have so much to offer right here in our fellowship.

- Waste your education out in the middle of nowhere? What will your dad say? After all, he paid the bill for your college degree!

- Why don't you get a good job here? Make some money so you'll be secure; later on you can think about getting involved in missions. Or, just give your money to someone else to go.

- You can't hurt your mother that way! How can you take her grandkids away from her? They need her!

- What about your kids' education? They will come home unprepared for college. How will they ever fit in back here socially?

- You expect to get married out there? You'll never meet anybody!

In a final lament, abandoning all attempts at logic, they may cry, "I don't believe this is happening to *me!*"

The cross-cultural worker who has already battled it out with the Lord over feelings of inadequacy sits in a disheveled heap—beneath a pile of stones, battered and bruised—hurting. The few and the strong who make it, encourage themselves in the Lord. But it would be so much better if they had you as a part of their moral support team to encourage them.

> "You have so much to offer right here in our fellowship."

per Justin

younger generation more

Self-indulgent sleep is the state of too large a segment of today's Church. Self-indulgence has produced a myopic introspection; we seem to focus on healing ourselves so we can have better lives. "Lord, comfort me so I will be comfortable" is in direct contrast to what is said in 2 Corinthians 1:4 (and throughout Scripture).

We want to be comfortable and we want security. We feel uneasy about unpredictability—like Peter as he blurted out in his threatened loss of security, "Lord, I won't let You die" (Matthew 16:22)!

Our society's drive for the "Great American Dream" has become a nightmare! It keeps many potential moral supporters lulled in a stupor of spiritual inactivity. "Shop 'til I drop!" is the motto of too many well meaning, but misguided Christians.

"Our church can't afford another program."

Perhaps the "Barnabas and Saul" of your fellowship have completed a Perspectives Course (www.perspectives.org) or have come back from an Urbana Student Missions Conference (www.urbana.org), or maybe a three-week mini-mission or a summer of service sensing the greatness of God's plan of the ages and their privileged part in it. Perhaps in your church, as in too many others, few barely rouse themselves to hear these enthusiasts report on what God is doing globally. As the church nods off, the potential missionaries say, "Could you not listen to what I believe God has in store for us for just one minute? Please, listen to me."

The cross-cultural worker goes back to the Rock and prays again, "Father, there must be some other way for You to accomplish Your purpose than by having me go."

"No, My child. This is the way. Walk ye in it" (Isaiah 30:21). And his hour comes. No support is given. All scatter. And the cross-cultural worker faces the Judases and priests and mobs of this world on his own—unless you are there to give him your moral support.

Worries about public opinion can hurt a missionary. Perhaps the potential cross-cultural worker is told, "Okay, if you have to go, go. But don't rock the boat. Don't get the people here involved—especially financially. Our church cannot afford another program!" Fortunately, it is getting harder and harder for churches to have this attitude because more and more mission organizations and those agencies helping to prepare cross-cultural workers for service are insisting that the local fellowship take the initiative in the missions process.

A mission agency, headquartered on the eastern coast of America, observed an awakening in churches to take a more active role in world evangelization. A seasoned missionary was asked by this agency to head up and develop a new division: Church Relations. He was given a clear, but open mandate to help churches reengage in the missions process. He called me. "Where is a good starting point?" he asked. I shared my belief that the easiest and most effective entry level for churches is member care—developing a partnership team of individuals to provide the primary care for each missionary family—to become "partners in the Gospel," as Paul commended the Christian in Philippi for their support. (Download a free DVD, *Partners in the Gospel* at the ACTS Media Library: www.eri.org.)

And here was the plan he proposed: The agency was soon to begin orientation training for seventeen candidate families. The agency would invite and pay for the seventeen senior pastors of their home churches to join the candidates for a seminar weekend. I poured the passion of my heart into the minds of those people planning to go to the front lines of spiritual warfare. And into the minds of their pastors.

The following day, I had a meeting with just the seventeen pastors. Anticipating a negative response from a few, my first words were, "I don't want a single one of you to say, 'This won't work in my church.' The agency has made it perfectly clear that they are giving you the 'lion's share' of the responsibilities of member care. You will have to find a way to make it work in your church." (In writing, that sounds a bit harsher than it was in person!) From that beginning a very positive atmosphere emerged. We had a good discussion of issues and ways to overcome many difficulties. (The one that seemed to distress them the most: We have never done it this way before!)

That agency continues to educate their missionaries' churches in their privileged position to take the primary role in member care.

However, sadly, there are still thousands of cases in which a mission candidate's pastor is the "last to know." Or perhaps he never finds out! Public opinion in some churches does not allow for radical moves into international evangelization. So the cross-cultural worker has to leave very quietly— unless you are there to shout an encouraging, "Bon voyage!"

"We have never done it this way before!"

Other attitudes can also dry up your cross-cultural worker's supply of moral support.

Competition within the Body of Christ scares some fellowships into undermining a mission candidate's moral support. The message might be very strong: "We don't want to lose you."

It wasn't that the Jews did not believe in world evangelization. For Christ said of them, "You travel over land and sea to make one convert" (Matthew 23:15). Nor was it that they were against His healing people. But throngs of people were following Jesus; He was a threat to the establishment. He was the competition; He didn't fit into their programs.

The bold, the daring, the aggressive plans of the world missionary community don't fit into the programs of many of today's churches, either—unless you are there to trumpet Christ's command of "Go into *all* the world...."

Contradictory counsel can discourage a missionary. The Apostle Paul sensed at every turn the potential of the enemy's

move. "I will stay in Ephesus until Pentecost, for God has
opened a great and effectual door, *and* with many adversaries"
(1 Corinthians 16:8-9). At Miletus he wrote, "I am compelled
by the Spirit to go to Jerusalem. I don't know what may
happen to me there, except that the Holy Spirit warns me that
imprisonment and persecution await me in every city that I
visit" (Acts 20:22-23).

So when the disciples in Caesarea said to Paul that he
should not go up to Jerusalem, he had to defend his certainty of
God's direction. Instead of receiving support, he had to rebuke
his friends: "What do you mean by unnerving me with all your
tears. You are breaking my heart! I am not only ready to be
bound, but to die for the sake of the name of the Lord Jesus."

Luke wrote, "And when we could not dissuade [Paul], we
held our tongues and said, 'The Lord's will be done!'" (Acts
21:13-14). You've probably seen it: The raised eyebrows, the
shrugged shoulders, the anxious look, all saying, "Just wait—
you'll see. We tried to warn you!"

And the one who is boldly doing the work of the Lord is left
alone—unless you are there to provide moral support to sustain
your missionary in his difficult times when even his friends are
opposing him.

Distorted theological views can end up damaging the morale
of a cross-cultural worker. The missionary heart of God is pierced
again and again as fellowships deny the Biblical injunctions to
go preach and teach.

Some shout it as brashly as did William Carey's
contemporaries: "God will do it without us if He wants it done!"
Others say it more subtly: "We're too young as a fellowship.
We're not big enough yet. No one in our fellowship seems
interested. We don't have the resources to support a missionary.
We don't have the time to devote to another new project. We
would only want to send our best, and we can't afford to lose
our leadership. There is so much that needs to be done here.
Why go somewhere else when the needs here are so great?"

Those excuses and a thousand more have all been thought

or spoken. Yet not a one of them stands the test of exposure to Scripture. Each excuse shrinks into the shadows, trying to hide from the Light of His Word. There is no theology to deny the missionary heartbeat of our God Who is "not willing that any perish, but that all come to repentance" (2 Peter 3:9)!

One year after Albania was freed from the tyrannical dictator who had claimed his country was totally atheistic, a new Albanian church of twenty members sent out their first cross-cultural missionary! No church is too young or small to ignore the call of God to cross-cultural outreach ministry. Time and again, senior pastors have turned their pulpit over to an assistant and have devoted their lives to cross-cultural ministry. Their action was not unlike that of the Antioch church, which sent out Barnabas and Saul.

Dan had heard the call of God on his life to go. He had visited Thailand on several occasions. There he had seen the hunger of pastors to learn how to study the Word. He had experienced the joy of helping them satisfy that hunger through the seminars he taught.

And now Dan was sure God was directing him to a longer-term commitment: to establish a ministry of conducting seminars for national pastors in Asia. These seminars would train them in the study of the Word, thus allowing them to better feed their flocks.

But Dan was the pastor of a church in the United States. It would not be easy to leave the people. He had founded the church. Who would fill his position? How could he uproot his family and move them into the unknown?

> "The entire congregation gave their full moral support."

What about the finances and logistics of that move? What about communication and prayer? Where would they stay when they came home?

All of these questions and apprehensions were real and needed answers. But they were more easily handled because the entire congregation gave their full moral support to what they sensed from the Lord to be a "new thing" for Dan and for them!

Yet, in too many churches, the cross-cultural parts of the Body—and there are cross-cultural parts, or else it is not a Body—hang lifeless in atrophy for lack of exercise. Or, if they are challenged by another church or agency, their home church is jealous because they are drawn away. And we are all the losers for it.

The story is told of a young sailor who was making final preparations for a solo voyage around the world in his homemade craft. Throngs of people crowded the small mooring as he stowed the last boxes of provisions. A murmuring air of pessimistic concern exploded into a volume of discouragement: "Son, you'll never make it! That boat will not withstand the waves of the storms! You'll run out of food! The sun will broil you!"

A late arriver, hearing all of these discouraging warnings, felt an irresistible desire to offer some optimism and encouragement. As the little craft began sailing away from the pier, he pushed his way to the end of the dock. Waving his hands wildly, he kept shouting, "Bon voyage! You're really somebody! We're with you! We're proud of you! God be with you, brother!"

Goede Reis!
Boa Viagem!
Sretan Put!
BON VOYAGE!
Nesi'a Tova!
Selamat Jalan!
Siwrne Dda!

The world seems to offer two kinds of support: "Wait 'til you get out in that cold, cruel world. It's rough!" And those who exude a contagious, confident "Bon voyage!"

There are dozens of thoughtless ways to burst the balloon of your aspiring missionary. But there are also plenty of ways you can buoy up his enthusiasm with solid moral support. In whatever language you say it, by whatever means you communicate it, be there to give your friend moral support through *every* stage of his missions experience.

Some Holy Spirit-guided soul-searching of your own attitudes toward cross-cultural ministry would be good at this point. An initial clearing away of any of these or other negative thoughts and actions will allow you to lay a foundation for building a strong support system for the cross-cultural outreach ministry of your church.

HOW TO GIVE SOLID-AS-A-ROCK MORAL SUPPORT

Moral support is the foundation of the sending process. Moral support is the "Bon voyage" of those who serve as senders to those who go. Moral support is as much an attitude that your cross-cultural worker will sense as it is an action you can do. And, by your actions, they will sense your attitude! Let's look at some solid foundation stones.

Jesus is the Chief Cornerstone. There first, of course, has to be a cornerstone, "... a tried stone, a precious cornerstone, a sure foundation" (Isaiah 28:16). In Jesus' day, the cornerstone was not some memorial plaque mortared into the wall after the building was completed. It was the first stone set. All measurements of height, length and breadth were taken from it. If it were well placed, the building had a good chance of being well constructed. But if it were poorly laid, watch out!

Christ's life and teachings were an example of moral support. In fact, when Matthew wrote his Gospel, the Holy Spirit inspired him to recall how Jesus fulfilled Isaiah's prophecy: "The bruised reed shall He not break, and the smoking (dimly burning) flax shall He not quench" (Matthew 12:20, quoting Isaiah 42:3). A more current rendering is, "He does not crush the weak, nor snuff out the smallest candle flame." "He doesn't kick you when you're down!" might be an appropriate paraphrase.

What does He do?

He takes the bruised reed by the hand, lifts her up, and says, "Where are your accusers? Has no one condemned you? Neither do I condemn you. Go and sin no more" (John 8:1-11)! He meets the "smoking flax" at night since Nicodemus feared the Jews. He gently breathes the Spirit of Life into that newly burning soul (John 3:1-21). Peter's tears of remorse had all but extinguished his flame of fire. Jesus tenderly fans those failing embers back to life with His trilogy of poignant questions: "Peter, do you love Me? Feed My sheep" (John 21:15-18)!

His example of refusing to condemn and determining to encourage is the cornerstone of our support structure as we serve as senders. But it's not enough just to do His deeds. No amount of human-level determination will equip you to be an adequate sender if you're not an intimate disciple of Jesus Christ. This topic is beyond our focus of study, but every sender, every sending team must be personally, constantly communing with the One Who in moral support told us, "As My Father has sent Me, even so send I you" (John 20:21). And, "I will be with you always" (Matthew 28:20). *The Jesus Style*, a book by Gayle D. Erwin gives valuable and practical instruction on this subject.

The Simplicity of Moral Support. The cornerstone has been laid. He is Jesus Christ. We can begin building. The first foundation stone that nudges right up and fits so perfectly beside the Chief Cornerstone is the moral support of the church that helps cross-cultural workers to "Do it simply—and simply do it!"

Jesus was a master at reducing to simplicity the impassioned issues of His day—and ours.

On the complex issue of taxation, He said, "Whose image is on the coin?"

"Caesar's," was the answer.

"Well, you had better give it to him then. But also give to God what belongs to Him" (Luke 20:21-25)!

We spend hours questioning what life is all about. Where did we come from? Jesus simply said, "I came from the Father." We spend days wondering why we're here. Jesus said, "I am doing the will of the Father." We spend years worrying where we're going. Jesus said, "I am going to the Father." In simple yet precise terms, He answered the three universal questions of life! (Read John 13:1-15. Also, a free download teaching on these verses, titled *Servant-Leader*, is available at ERI's website: www.eri.org; ACTS Media Library.)

Jesus' ministry was deep, yet simple. And His lifestyle was also simple. He was born in a stable. He had no place to call home. His body occupied a borrowed tomb at His death.

As your cross-cultural worker begins taking the steps toward the fields of the world, a thousand opportunities and ways to minister will begin bombarding him. Encourage him to keep his eyes focused on the simple, straightforward ministry of Jesus. Urge him to listen quietly to the direction of the Spirit out of all the godly counsel he is receiving (Proverbs 19:20-21). Remind him to keep it simple; he's not some new messiah! Advise him also to simply do it—to keep going one step at a time.

Help him practice a "wartime lifestyle" even before going to the field. This doesn't mean living under an austere, ascetic vow of poverty. It means trimming off what isn't necessary. It means not spending on some things and spending strategically on others—much as a soldier going into combat doesn't need a gold-embossed jogging suit but does need a very expensive, state-of-the-art rifle.

Encouraging simplicity in ministry goals and in lifestyle is moral support! And for us to practice the same would be moral support, par excellence! Do we need a new outfit for every occasion? Or a Starbucks every day?

Read Dr. Ralph Winter's article, *Reconsecration To A Wartime Lifestyle*, to challenge your lifestyle in support of your missionary friend (www.reconsecration.org).

One frugal sender soaks and smooths the tiny last part of a bar of soap onto the new one. Admittedly, this does not save much money, if any. However, it serves him as a clear reminder of the importance of checking his expenditures in other areas.

Integrating Missions. The next foundation stone also fits snugly into its place. Support your worker in his perspective that mission is an integrated ministry of the church. Cross-cultural outreach is not the only God-ordained ministry.

"Yes, it is exciting to see that God has chosen you to minister cross-culturally. Yes, the zeal of the Lord is upon you," you can agree with your missionary friend. But then you may need to remind him that the Sunday school teachers who tolerated his elementary distractions are now dealing with the next generation of field workers. Therefore, their work continues to be vital. Or ask your friend when he last thanked the custodian for cleaning the church restrooms.

All the parts of the Body work together in one direction within the "unchangeable purpose of God" (Hebrews 6:11-18), each adding its own expertise. Some of these ministries are more direct in the ultimate purpose of the Church—to bless with the Good News every people, tribe and tongue. And some are indirectly related, yet as vital to the whole.

The *life* of the Church is worship. Therefore, those in the Body who lead us into the presence of God function well to teach us all forms of worship. The *growth* of the Church is nurture. Therefore, those in the Body who "rightly divide the Word of Truth" (II Timothy 2:15)

> "The *mission* of the Church is outreach."

for us do well to "devote themselves to the study of God's Word and prayer" (Acts 6:4). Further, the *mission* of the Church is outreach. Reaching out to "Jerusalem, Judea, Samaria, and to the uttermost parts." Whether it is to the neighbor next door, the hardened criminal in prison or a "hidden" people group in Papua New Guinea, reaching out to the lost is the mission of the church. (A free download, *The Mission of the Church,* is available at ERI's ACTS Media Library.)

Unfortunately, however, it seems like the "uttermost parts"—the cross-cultural outreach is the most lacking (under-focused, even ignored) ministry of a church. You can help to bring a focus to cross-cultural outreach ministry by integrating an awareness of it through all of the ministries of the church. For example, encourage the worship leaders to incorporate missions-challenging songs from time to time. Provide cross-cultural illustrations to your pastor that would fit with his sermon series. Check with the Children and Youth Ministers that scores of opportunities to integrate cross-cultural awareness are being provided for them.

Donna is able to share a "Missions Minute" (which expanded to 10-15 minutes) each Sunday morning. Heidi has five to ten minutes once a month to highlight a missionary or mission resource—sometimes showing a PowerPoint or video clip. You can encourage your missionary to remember that an accurate, big-picture worldview integrates ministries; it doesn't eliminate some nor value one ministry above another. You, your missionary friend and all involved in cross-cultural outreach ministry are thus helped to keep a proper perspective on missions.

This is not easy for a missionary to appreciate as he gets into his ministry. His part of the big picture of God's purpose can easily become the only activity he sees. Therefore, you enter as his moral supporter to give him a Godly perspective. You are able to help him recognize that moral support is a two-way street: To enjoy the moral support of others demands that he be interested in and be an encouragement to them in their endeavors.

Active Listening. Another foundation stone of moral support is the art of active listening. Paul Tournier in his book *To Understand Each Other* said, "Most conversations of this world are 'dialogues of the deaf.'" Emotional isolation is already a major problem in North America. And the mass movement to "social interaction" via the Internet further denies the value of active listening. Whether talking to a machine on the telephone which recognizes your voice prompts or "chatting" by written words on your computer screen, active listening is not happening. When we have to be advised to not "flush the toilet" while we are talking with a prospective employer, we have skidded down a very slippery slide to a lack of active listening. So when your friend is grappling with all the uncertainties of moving into cross-cultural outreach ministry, he needs even greater support: he needs your listening ear.

When your friend shares his thoughts about cross-cultural involvement, your ministry of moral support is most effective as you simply sit and listen—actively.

Active listening is probably one of the most neglected foundation stones of moral support. Active listening says, "I am with you. I will take the time. I will put energy into really listening to your heart, not only to what your words are saying." Active listening also "hears" what you are *not* saying.

Active listening calls for all of your attention. It is hard work; it requires concentration. But how necessary it is to moral support!

Active listening obligates you to respond with respect. You do not "own" his feelings, but you allow him to have his perspective. Through your conversation you reflect your consideration of his position.

Active listening expresses empathy. Even though you are not "in his shoes" and cannot fully comprehend what he is experiencing, you can try to sense his thoughts and feelings as he anticipates his venture of faith.

Active listening demands that you give feedback. Repeat in your own words what you believe you heard him say. For example, imagine yourself listening to Scott and Jean after their traumatic meeting with Pastor Joe as recounted at the beginning of this chapter:

Scott says, "Then Pastor Joe spoke and said, 'I have made the decision that you are not to continue in this mission!' Man, we were stunned!"

You say, "I guess so!" Expressing your own surprise.

"No kidding," says Jean. "I guess our objections were not too well thought-out."

You say, "You mean your objections to his objections?"

Jean laughs. "Yeah, I guess so. What we said probably didn't make much sense since we were so confused."

You say, "Your thoughts were too scattered to explain to him how you knew God wants you to go."

"Right," says Scott. "We sure know how to explain it to people now after that experience!"

You say, "Feels good to be confident about God's direction, doesn't it?"

Jean says, "It sure does—even in spite of Pastor Joe's response. ..."

And you've effectively listened through a painful experience that needed to be shared. Further, you've also allowed Scott and Jean to work through some of their feelings about the incident until they begin to have some positive feelings about it.

Your active listening and repeating in your own words what you thought you heard results in a great show of solid moral support! Just being there to listen with positive feedback helps your missionary clarify his thoughts and feelings on a host of new concepts he must process.

We all know the risks of international travel. We all know the dangers of terrorist activity. We all know the socio-political issues concerning the rise in nationalism. We all know the fears of the unknown. God does, too. Yet He says, "Go!"

Will you be one of those who will say, "Wow! What a privilege to be about our Father's business!"? Will you offer, "We're with you! What can we do to help?" Will you be the one who shouts, "God bless you! We're proud of you! You're really something! Bon voyage!"?

Stone by stone, the foundation of moral support is being laid.

Commissioning as Moral Support. There may be other stones of solid moral support that His Spirit will bring to your mind. But for now let's consider just three more stones that are vital to this foundation: confirmation, strategy determined and commissioned. The church in Antioch provides a model from which we can draw our examples.

They put five men forward; they fasted and prayed. They heard the Holy Spirit say, "We want Barnabas and Saul." They fasted and prayed some more. They laid their hands on them. They sent them away. Who is "they"? The church, the local Body of believers—those who were sharing their own concern for this ministry that was burning deep in the hearts of Barnabas and Saul.

- Confirmation. The church, the home fellowship, the missions fellowship, the prayer group, the college and career class, the "over fifties" bunch—some group besides the one wanting to go needs to hear the Holy Spirit say, "Separate unto Me [the Barnabas and Saul from your fellowship] for the task to which I have called them" (Acts 13:2). This confirmation provides tremendous moral support! It is one thing for your missionary to think the Lord has directed him. It is incredibly more reassuring to know He has confirmed it in the hearts of others as well.

- Strategy Determined. The church fasted and prayed some more (Acts 13:3). Though Scripture isn't specific, it would seem logical that they were seeking guidance from the Lord for details of this new venture. The passage implies that a group larger than the two going heard answers to these questions: How should they go? Where is the money coming from? What do they take with them? When should they go? What are they going to do when they get there? Where is "there" (Matthew 10:1-16)?

This was a new beginning as this team of senders determined how they could best be supportive to some of the Church's first missionaries. Remember, the Antioch church was filled with people just like you and me. They were able to carry the weight of these unprecedented decisions as a team of people who had, in fasting and prayer, heard the Lord's direction. So can we today!

- Commissioned. The senders laid their hands on the missionaries (Acts 13:3).

In Hebrews 6, the laying on of hands is named as one of the foundational doctrines. In this situation, the event was a commissioning, a setting-apart for a specific task, an identifying with the upcoming ministry of the sent ones.

Whether your cross-cultural worker is going short-term or longer, he needs the spiritual covering—the moral support—of "the laying on of hands," because, as an extension of your church's ministry, he is going out to battle against the enemy. As the "feet" in the Body of Christ, he is representing your whole body (Acts 10:15).

Though my attitude before arriving at the church was not as it should have been (it was a hot, Sunday afternoon—time to be at the beach), a commissioning service I attended became for me (and for the missionaries) a highlight to be remembered. The church was packed, many standing along the side walls. As expected, the elders had the couple stand

"A commissioning service for the goers *and* the senders."

before them in the front. The head elder asked them a series of questions regarding their commitment to the work on the field. To each question, they answered, "We will." Then, to my amazement, the elders had the congregation stand. Another series of questions was asked of the congregation, to which they were to respond audibly. A commissioning service for both the goers and the senders!

Trying to understand your missionary, of course, means that you'll need to do some fine-tuning of your understanding of what he'll be facing. You need to know what God is doing these days in cross-cultural outreach ministry.

Many of these classics are available today as ebooks. Read how Jackie Pullinger broke through the Walled City of Hong Kong in *Chasing the Dragon*. Marvel at how a 19-year-old touched the lives of Latin American Indians in *Bruchko* by Bruce Olson. Weep in sorrow at the price Christ paid for the lost of Russia as you read *Vanya* by Myrna Grant or *Tortured For His Faith* by Haralan Popov. Understand the cost of commitment in Pakistani Muslim Bilquis Sheikh's *I Dared to Call Him Father*. F. Kefa Sempangi gives a first person account of the martyrdom of Christians in Uganda in *A Distant Grief*, and follows that with *From the Dust, A Sequel*. Rejoice that God has placed *Eternity in Their Hearts* as examined in Don Richardson's book on redemptive analogy, a key to proclaiming Christ to the nations. Brian Hogan's biographical account of

God's movement in Mongolia is humorously, yet seriously told in *There's a Sheep in My Bathtub*. *Which None Can Shut* by Reema Goode tells remarkable stories of God's miraculous work in the Muslim world. What it means to be a Christian in Vietnam is told by Reg Reimer in *Vietnam's Christians*. Beyond these, the Internet is overflowing with accounts of God's eternal plan through servants who have responded to His call as has your missionary friend. Just Google "missionary blog" and you will have a plethora of information. Facebook? Twitter? Yes, if you "dare!" Become an expert on the steady progress of the 21st century's Great Commission endeavor.

As you identify with your missionary's work, what you learn about God's work around the world will bring a deeper sense of your part in God's global purpose and of how your role is critical as you give moral support to those who say, "I think God wants me to be a missionary! And I want you, church, to send me!"

It Happened This Way in Pennsylvania

A senior pastor was a member of the Board of Directors of a mission agency. That agency had just received their custom edition of the book, *Serving As Senders*. (This allowed them to have their logo on the cover, their organization's name on the Title Page and their endorsements on the back cover. But, most importantly, they had me rewrite Chapter Eight, "Your Part in the Big Picture." They gave me the material to tell their specific "part" in the Big Picture. Custom editions of this book can still be published.)

Pastor Mike received his copy. He drove home after the meeting. Late into the night he drove. And, while driving, he read the book! This is not recommended! You are discovering that it is a very valuable book, but not so important as to risk an auto accident.

The next day, Pastor Mike had his secretary write up a Letter of Resignation for each of his Mission Committee members. He ordered a case of the books. He called a meeting. Without hesitation or explanation, he handed to each of them their personal Letter of Resignation. And said, "Sign it!"

Not knowing what he was up to, yet knowing his propensity for the unusual, they each signed their Letter. "You know that by signing this Letter that you are no longer a member of the Missions Committee that has guided our church for these many years?" he asked. But it was more a statement of fact! Hesitant agreement came with each nod of very perplexed heads. With the last member's assent, Pastor Mike said, "Good! You are now all appointed to a new Missions Committee. For, you see, we are not going to be doing missions the same way anymore." He waited until they had read their copy of the book before calling the next meeting.

The church had 34 missionary families. They were all "home grown", i.e., were members of that fellowship, were known by the people and had been active in ministry before the church sent them out. Excitement grew as the "word" got out that more people were needed to engage in the missions process. It was not difficult to begin identifying core leadership.

Thirty-four leadership teams were formed. They called them Quest Teams. In cooperation with the missionary families, the various coordinators contacted people who had shown some interest in their specific mission. Prayer became more specific. No longer the "God bless our missionaries, wherever they are." Through the Quest Team Prayer Coordinator people were kept informed of specific needs and praise reports. Knowing that Updates would be read, the missionaries were more diligent in getting their reports to the Communication Coordinator. People took more interest in caring for the families when they came home. The teams took "ownership" of a more focused ministry. Their missionary's vision was becoming their passion, as well.

After about two years, they called me. Pastor Mike told me of the effectiveness of the coordination efforts provided by the Quest Teams. He asked if I would come and do a "super-charged" seminar just for the Quest Teams. It was my pleasure!

Moral support is obviously basic if you're serving as a sender. Maybe your forte as a sender will be boosting your missionary's morale. Do you always see the glass "half full"? Can you easily put an encouraging word in an appropriate context? Do you think you can develop this skill?

But other phases of support are important, too, if your sent-one is going to be fully supported. Somebody has to help with the nuts and bolts, the "thousands" of details to be considered while your friend is preparing to go, while he is on the field and when he returns home. In the next chapter, we will see that missionaries need careful, solid logistics support.

(In addition to the individual study below, see the **Group Leader's Guide** for Chapter Two beginning on page 200.)

FOR YOUR PERSONAL INVOLVEMENT

- Read Matthew 12:20 from a number of translations. Choose one that really communicates the message to you. Memorize it. Meditate on it. Allow the Holy Spirit to infuse this concept of moral support into the very fiber of your being.

- Read, in its context, the story of each of the individuals in the Bible we referred to. Place next to their names the relationship of the people who could have been of moral support to them:

    David, 1 Samuel 30 _____

    Jesus, Luke 22 _____

    Mary, Matthew 1 _____

    The blind man, John 9 _____

    Paul, Acts 21 _____

- Choose one of the stories. In your own words, retell the story as if those people had given moral support.

- Because moral support is a two-way street, it would be interesting to survey your Sunday school teachers with the question: "When our missionaries have been home for an extended time, have any of them ever thanked you for teaching our kids? Have you ever thanked them for representing us in cross-cultural ministry?" Share your survey results with your pastor.

- Review the six attitudes and actions that do not provide support. Ask the Lord (and then listen to His answer) if there is a root of any of them in you. Search the Scriptures for solutions to rid yourself of them.

- What are some Biblical proverbs to govern our actions in moral support? (Ex: Pro 25:11)

ACTION STEPS

By the time you have read Chapter Two, completed the *For Your Personal Involvement* section and participated in a discussion group, you should ...

- Understand that moral support is the basic foundation of the support system.

- Express appreciation and give moral support to everyone in the fellowship who is a functioning part of the Body. (When *is* the last time anyone in the church thanked the custodian for cleaning the toilets? Have you?)

- Realize that moral support is an ongoing relationship with your missionary, and that it is as easily sensed by your actions of support as by your words.

- Write to one of your missionaries on the field and say, "Here is my belated 'Bon voyage!' God bless you!"

- Multiply yourself. You might be surprised how contagious enthusiastic moral support becomes! Encourage others with your practice of encouragement!

CHAPTER 3

Logistics Support

**"And when you come, please bring the cloak I left
with Carpus at Troas and the books, but especially the
parchments."**
2 Timothy 4:13

"SURE, I HAD had some good training in developing a partnership team. I had made provision for my logistics support. A great guy named Bill had said he would handle everything. Looking back, that should have been my first clue that this might not work out. Nobody can handle everything! But I didn't think of it at the time.

"A ministry opportunity had opened up. We had been invited to lead a relief work in the Middle East. We sensed God's direction in this. Things were coming together well. A lot of clothes and medicine were being given to us to distribute once we got there. We neatly packed and identified each box. Bill said that when sailors from our church came to a nearby military installation, he would have them each carry a few of the boxes. Or he was sure he could arrange space for the whole shipment through diplomatic channels. What a relief to my mind; I could concentrate on other details.

"Three years later, we came home for a short visit. I sheepishly went to the friend who had let us store those boxes

in his garage, lo, these three years. Yes! They were all there—
just as we had left them! Not a one had been sent to us.

"We shipped the stuff to a ministry in Mexico. They said
they could use what wasn't outdated. I took the few remaining
boxes of our personal items to Bill. 'Yeah, sure! No problem.
Those will be on the next ship out!' Yes! We trusted him again.

"Well, we're ready to come home on furlough again. We've
decided that since we've made it for six years over here without
that stuff, we really don't need it. It will be interesting, though,
when we get home to look through the boxes to see what one
day had seemed so important to us.

"Bill's a good man. But he just didn't seem to be able to get
those boxes over to us!"

Logistics support deals with handling the nuts and bolts
of your cross-cultural worker's continuing home country
responsibilities.

Logistics support must be considered on two levels: 1) Those
areas of business to be attended to by the church leadership
or mission agency, and 2) the multitude of details that can be
handled by a team of individuals. You, as part of the logistics
support team, could find yourself involved in:

- Identifying the cross-cultural workers in your fellowship.
- Maintaining their accountability in ministry.
- Confirming and encouraging their spiritual growth.
- Managing their business affairs.
- Attending to various personal needs of your missionary
  friend.

IDENTIFYING CROSS-CULTURAL WORKERS

The local congregation, the Body of Christ in microcosm,
must have all the necessary parts in order to function as a Body.
The Body needs a mouth, so He appointed some prophets, some
pastors and teachers. The Body needs to function "decently and

in order," so He gave some the gift of administration. He even has someone always "just hanging around," like the appendix! (We joke about the appendix, but science has discovered its value to the immune system.)

Since outreach is one of the main functions of the Church, and because He said, "The field is the world" (Matthew 13:38), God has placed in every Body, parts that are to minister cross-culturally.

In many churches, cross-cultural workers have not been given the opportunity to exercise their gifts, so they just sit around in atrophy, wondering, "Why am I here?" "What is my purpose in this fellowship?" They may try to find a place of ministry in an area, but they just don't fit in! So in frustration they move from one ministry to another—even from one church to another.

The first logistical responsibility of the church, then, is to provide for the identification and exercise of its cross-cultural parts.

When Barnabas and Saul returned to Antioch from Jerusalem with some firsthand reports from the Apostles, the *church* identified and put forth five men—prophets and teachers, leaders in the church. Then, in prayer and fasting, the *church* heard the Holy Spirit say, "I want Barnabas and Saul for some cross-cultural work." (A rather loose paraphrase of Acts 13:1-2!)

The local fellowship of believers must take the initiative in the missionary process by identifying the cross-cultural parts of the Body and allowing them to exercise their gifts.

A missions fellowship at your church, then, becomes an ideal testing ground for potential missionaries and senders. Under the direction of a lay or staff leader, those who believe they are your Body's cross-cultural parts can experience all aspects of missions. They can be challenged to the task of cross-cultural outreach ministry by speakers, cultural studies and reports, motivational and training DVDs and by relating with missionaries who are home. They can practice the skills of missionary support—moral, logistics, prayer, finance, communication and reentry. They can exercise their gifts by ministering to the internationals in your own hometown. As potential *goers* are identified, they can actually go on a mini-mission or short-term experience. And the identified *senders* can serve as their senders!

The pastor, church or missions committee should not be the last to know when one of the members from your Body is getting involved in missions! Make cross-cultural outreach a part of the vision God has given for your fellowship. And provide a venue through which these gifts can be exercised.

MAINTAINING ACCOUNTABILITY IN MINISTRY

Accountability—being responsible to someone for your actions—is a concept that cycles through time and cultures. Anchored in Biblical Truth, it is a principle Christians understand. Yet, from across the nation, there are hundreds of pastors and church leaders who do not know what those who have gone out from their church are doing. Some say, "Well, they're with XYZ Ministry. Isn't that a good mission?"

Quite possibly, but there are questions to be asked and answers to be understood before your missionary goes:

- Is that mission an extension of the ministry goals of your church?

- Is that ministry targeting a decisive point of battle—one worth doing and having the necessary resources available to do it?

- Are your missionary's abilities and giftings suited to the work of that mission?

A second dimension of this responsibility then follows: Once you are sure your cross-cultural worker is involved in a ministry suited to his gifts and the ministry thrust of your church, you must have some on-going evaluation to know how your worker is progressing. A regular, independent report from his supervisor will keep you in touch with his work.

If your missionary is working through a mission agency,

make sure the lines of accountability relationship are open, defined and that they include your fellowship. It is an out-dated mindset that once a missionary "joins" an agency, the church has no further involvement with him. Remember, this missionary is still a part of your Body! According to Romans 10:15 (quoting Isaiah 52:7), missionaries could be likened to the "feet" in the Body of Christ. When our (physical) feet go somewhere, our whole body goes! And the same should be true of the Body of Christ. You, the church, are going with your missionary, not in person, but certainly in spirit.

One mission committee chairman lamented: "We sent them out to fulfill a responsibility that they were well suited for. We knew they would do well. And they did. After a few months, the field leadership put the husband in another position for which he and his wife argued that he was not qualified: Regional finance. He cried, "I don't even know

> "Regular contact with your worker is vital."

how to balance a check book!" But he submitted. The finance director, who had to go home for heart surgery, showed him around the first day, promising to stay until he understood the job. However, that night he died of a heart attack, leaving this once-happy man to fend for himself through a maze of figures and forms. When he 'really messed up', they sent him home 'a failure'."

Regular contact with your worker will prevent this from happening. One missions chairman calls his field workers every week. Nothing long or detailed—just, "How are you doing today?" Possibly *you* could shoulder that responsibility!

A formal report from your worker could keep you informed. I have seen some forms that have been prepared for this purpose. Minute detail! But, unfortunately, everybody knows the "right" answer to give! I believe that person-to-person, informal talking is still the best way to relate with your missionaries. I repeat: a periodic phone call or even a visit by an appointed elder from your church would assure you that the ministry is really happening and your "feet" are in good condition. Modern communication methods—from email to Skype and beyond, make this reporting easier. However, there need to be people who will see that it is actually done. After all, the work of those who go and those who serve as senders is a team effort!

CONFIRMING SPIRITUAL GROWTH

Sadly, some sets of statistics report that for all their preparation, for all their "hearing God's voice" and for all their support, up to 50% of cross-cultural workers do not complete their first term of commitment or do not return for their second.

Too many of them don't make it because of spiritual drought. They have dried up spiritually. They have come to the point where they are trying to give out more than they are taking in.

Church leadership must encourage spiritual growth 1) before missionaries go, 2) while they're on the field and 3) when they return home.

1) Encouragement in spiritual growth before they go.

Antioch provides a good example: Barnabas and Saul were mature leaders chosen by the Holy Spirit for a very tough assignment. It is easy to study their fine qualifications in Scripture.

For some reason, however, they took John Mark along. Evidently he was not prepared; when the going got tough, he quit (Acts 13:13).

Several years later, Paul sensed that John Mark still was not ready (Acts 15:38). But then several years after that assessment, Paul told Timothy to bring Mark with him, for "he is profitable for the ministry" (2 Timothy 4:11).

A goer's eagerness to be sent doesn't necessarily mean he is ready to be sent. One young woman (19) was encouraged by her church leader to "just go!" A seasoned missionary had told me that he was encouraging her to get some pre-field training. She called me. 'Good,' I thought. 'She will fit into our next Course.' "Oh, no!" she objected. "I leave tomorrow. I just have one question: When I arrive in Abuja, Nigeria, do I ask the American Embassy to pick me up?"

One church does it this way: Everyone who even thinks he is a cross-cultural part of the Body is encouraged to attend the missions fellowship headed by the cross-cultural coordinator. Here they are regularly exposed to cross-cultural outreach through prayer for the peoples of the world. Speakers and DVDs and YouTube clips and Internet profiles of ministries and opportunities for ministry are available to challenge the group. Short-term awareness and ministry trips give the participants some first hand experience.

As this person (or couple) and the group sense the call of the potential goer, he begins relating with the senior pastor in personal discipleship training. Then he is raised to the position of deacon in the church and functions for a time in a position of leadership. His whole church has been watching

"The church must send workers who know what they believe and why."

and participating in his development. At some point, then, he is ready for cross-cultural training and developing a personal partnership team.

The church must send a capable, credible worker—one who knows what he believes and why. That confidence may come through in-house training, through a Bible college or a combination of several preparation programs.

The church must not send one who is "ever learning, yet never able to come to the knowledge of the truth" (2 Timothy 3:7), but one who is "increasing in the knowledge of God" (Colossians 1:10).

The church must send one who has stripped the Gospel and teachings of Christ of all American, Greek and Hebrew culture so that he can allow his host culture to clothe the Gospel in garb suitable to them. If a people group holds all of their important meetings under a large tree, does the missionary have to build a church—with a steeple? Let the church gatherings meet under a tree. (Unless, of course, there are pagan roots to that tree or that practice.)

The church must send one who has been trained in interpersonal relationships, the lack of which is the greatest reason for missionary dropouts! For, "they will know we are His disciples by our love *for one another*" (John 13:35). If the enemy is able to strike a blow in our getting along with each other, great damage can be done in our relationships with the people among whom we are ministering.

The church must send one who knows how to face spiritual warfare and live in the victory Christ has won for us on Calvary, so that he can aggressively engage in the battle for lost souls. (An in-depth study on this is available through the book, Prepare For Battle! or DVD seminar by the same title at www.eri.org.)

The church must send one who has learned how to live in a second culture. He must be sensitive, as a guest in their country to not trample on their lifestyles, yet to clearly present the Gospel in words and terms that make sense to them.

Every mission agency provides a time of orientation, but all do not as yet require a time of learning how to live and minister in a second culture. You want your "feet" to thrive in their field experience. Thus, you will insist that your worker has had adequate pre-field training.

2) Encouragement in spiritual growth on the field.

Once a field worker becomes unencumbered with the affairs of his life back home (2 Timothy 2:4) and is thrust into the midst of unending opportunity for ministry, it is very easy for him to neglect his own spiritual intake—to be working so hard *for* the Lord that he neglects his personal relationship *with* the Lord. Soon yesterday's prayers, last week's Bible reading, last month's study in the Word are not able to sustain the worker through today's demands. Then he falls prey to spiritual drought.

Your worker doesn't have five Christian radio stations, two Christian TV stations and a dozen Bible studies to choose from each week. Therefore, he must be a student of the Word—

one who knows how to "rightly divide the Word of Truth, a workman who doesn't need to be ashamed" (2 Timothy 2:15). He must know how to feed himself spiritually.

You may help in this area by sending him your pastor's Bible study CDs, or by having him commit to a Bible course on the Internet. Perhaps you can study along with him by email or an on-line book-by-book Bible study.

When our family was in the jungles of Peru, we arranged for our church to send one of the pastor's weekly Bible study. Several families heard about them. Soon a group of team members joined us. Before long many groups were organized and listening to the pastor's Bible studies! When we heard new choruses being sung, we realized how much we missed our Christian music. We quickly got on the ham radio to ask a support team member to send some Christian music down—soon! Yes, a few regions of the world, even today, are not connected to the Internet! Or could be connected, but at such an expense as to make it prohibitive for frequent use.

3) Encouragement in spiritual growth when they come back home.

Your missionary may be home for a brief stay before he returns to the field. Check his spiritual temperature. He has been bombarded by new ideas and ideals, different values and beliefs. Is his "house" still founded on the Rock? Are the changes in his thinking only cultural? Or has a subtle pantheism or other deceptive world system outlook tainted his doctrine? He may need a strengthening of his faith. More seriously, he may need a redefining of his Christian foundations. Some slightly skewed winds of doctrine may have even come from the isolated team with which he was working.

You may also want to check the artifacts your missionary brings home. As curious as they may be, they may carry unwelcome problems if they had been used in demonic spirit worship. A sensitive grandma was babysitting for her daughter. The daughter had said that her child had recently begun having terrible nightmares. That evening, Grandma saw an evil idol sitting on the girl's shelf. She asked the mother when the nightmares began. Then, she asked when that statue had been placed in her room. Yes, at the same time. The mother just wanted to put it in a different room! Again, Grandma wisely said it had to be destroyed. The child stopped having nightmares! Oh, the curios can be so fascinating! And deadly! But you will be there for your friend to make sure no demonic artifacts have been brought home.

If your worker has come home to take up a new ministry here, you cannot presume that his spiritual growth will continue. Here at home he is bombarded by the gods of materialism and hedonism. These can have a drastic effect on his doctrine! Make sure he is still sharing what he "first received from the Lord" (1 Corinthians 15:3).

> **"Curios can be so fascinating! And deadly!"**

A certain family served on a two-year mission venture in the Orient. They returned to the States to resume ministry. It wasn't until much later—fifteen years later—through the counsel of their church leadership that they came to understand the intensity of a spiritual assault that had been launched against their whole family while on the field. They then began to work on breaking the powers of darkness and the resulting destructive patterns and began to live in the victorious freedom available in Christ. Supportive, intense prayer for them by the Body when they first came home might have identified this problem sooner. Unfortunately, then and even still today, too many are ignorant of the spiritual assaults of the enemy. Do not let this be true of your fellowship. Make sure you and your missionary friend know how to live in the victory Christ won for us on Calvary.

MANAGING BUSINESS AFFAIRS

If your worker goes through a mission agency, most of the following issues will be established by the agency's policy. Reading through some of these perplexing logistics might help you appreciate what an agency has to do to keep your missionary on the field. However, even if these tasks are handled by an agency, it is still your responsibility to know the agency's policies and how you as the sending church relate to them. More and more mission agencies are asking for the church to be more actively involved in the whole missions process—including logistics.

If your church sends out missionaries directly to work with national ministries or to plant churches in unreached groups, first think and plan very seriously through each of the following issues. And remember that this list is only a cursory look at all the business matters that will come up!

1) Money

This one word conjures up more emotion than any other in the whole arena of missions! Because of its importance, someone in the church leadership with the gift of administration must be responsible to handle its details:

a) Work with the national ministry and your cross-cultural worker to determine a necessary and adequate monthly budget. It is best to separate living and ministry expenses. Potential financial supporters need to know what is necessary for the missionary to *live* in a second culture and what is necessary to *minister* there. If it is just stated as a combined sum, people can wonder at how much the missionary needs as compared to their own "meager" wage!

b) Establish acceptable methods for securing enough financing. What will you do if donations fall below the established quota? What will you do if the dollar is devalued? What will you do if your missionary marries on the field? Has children?

c) Communicate clearly to the donor how to identify his gift. For instance, is the designation for a particular person or project? Checks in offering plates can too easily get misdirected into another category.

d) Develop a system for receipting the donor and for notifying your cross-cultural worker of the amounts and who donated. Include the donor's email address so his missionary can send a personal note of thanks. Careful financial monitoring is needed to actually transfer those funds to the field. Identity theft through Internet transfer of money can leave your missionary in deep debt. Also, will any percentage be kept back for administering the funding process?

Some churches believe the missionary should not know who is donating to their financial support, somehow using the Scripture, "... don't let your left hand know what your right hand is doing" (Matthew 6:3). However, we have known of givers quitting because they couldn't be sure their friend was receiving the funds because the gifts had not been acknowledged. Legally, the organization must reserve the right to use the funds at their discretion. This is for their tax purposes. However, most agencies will honor the designation made by the donor. You want to make sure your agency does.

Missionaries should be able to thank their donors. Jesus questioned where the nine were who did not come back to say "Thank You" (Luke 17:17). Read Paul's strong commendation to the Christians at Philippi for their generous, sacrificial gift (Philippians 4:10-19).

A computer program, such as QuickBooks, makes this a very clear and definitive process. There should be no "horror stories" here. Especially if you have the gift of administration and hear the Lord saying for you to step up to the task!

2) Taxes

How easily Jesus reduced to simplicity the whole issue of taxes (Matthew 22:15-22). Earthly governments, however, seem to be able to make things very complicated. Therefore "rendering unto Caesar" requires an astute mind knowledgeable of the myriads of details involved. Details such as deductions, tax status changes caused by your worker's ordination and length of residency outside the US, federal and state laws, and the host country's taxation just begin to open this Pandora's Box!

And, remember, tax laws are in a continual state of change. If your fellowship does not have the time to keep up with all the laws, find a tax professional who can help with your missionary's situation. It is imperative that you or someone from your church leadership contact them or some other truly knowledgeable financial organization before you send your worker to the field—just to make sure all is in order in this vital area of logistics support.

Mary was *just* going to Colombia for two years. "I won't be earning any money in the United States. I don't need to worry about taxes!" she thought. She discovered how wrong she had been when, after returning home, she got an invitation to explain why she hadn't filed her income tax forms for two years. Back taxes plus interest had her making painful payments for several years.

> **"I don't need to worry about taxes!"**

Or take John, who thought that because his church had written a letter, he didn't have to pay Social Security. Don't let your cross-cultural worker become a horror story of trouble with the government!

3) Health

Responsible church leadership will make sure their cross-cultural worker and his whole family are in good health—physically, emotionally, mentally and spiritually before they go to the field. Leadership must further see that their health care needs are met through an adequate monthly income or through the church's health insurance program.

Three considerations: 1) Will the church's policy cover your missionary family when they are out of the United States? 2) Is the cost of the premium higher than the cost of health care in the country to which they are going? 3) Is health care provided to expatriates by the host nation's medical program?

There is an excellent Scriptural way of meeting a missionary family's health care costs. It is not through an insurance company, but through a group of thousands of Christians who have committed to meet each other's medical needs. Millions of dollars have been exchanged as we "bear one another's burden" (Galatians 6:2). For more information contact Christian Healthcare Ministries: (800) 791-6225; www.chministries.org.

One missionary was receiving his funds through an agency that basically just handled his logistics needs. While he was on the field, that agency decided to change its insurance policy. Under the new program, everyone had to belong. Four hundred dollars more a month! That was half as much again of what they were currently receiving! Plus, he and his family were working in a country where their health care costs were covered by the local government. He had a decision to make. He chose to change agencies.

Definitely related to the health and well-being of your cross-cultural worker is his safety. What will you as a sending church do if your worker gets himself in trouble in his host culture? What if he is caught in the crossfire of a civil disturbance? What if the government is overthrown? What if your worker is kidnapped for ransom?

Has your missionary (and you) had training in crisis management? Even in such simple, practical measures called "target-hardening"? The organization to contact is Crisis Consulting International: (805) 642-2549; www.cricon.org.

Tragic are the stories of missionaries whose first thoughts about "what to do" come as the bullets are shooting off the lock on their door!

Some hard facts! It is far better, however, to have these issues thought out ahead of time and to have a plan of action in place than to wait for your worker's phone call from prison to begin thinking about such matters!

The list goes on.

4) Death

Death is an inevitable fact of life. Yet this most emotionally charged event is sometimes totally unplanned for by a missionary's sending church. To clarify the necessary details, your fellowship must plan ahead.

It is generally accepted that the best place to be buried is where one dies. Many countries do not embalm; therefore they require burial within 24 hours. The expense of immediate or even chartered flights out of a country are usually prohibitive. Furthermore, "He lived, he worked, he died and he is buried among us," is a powerful statement of the incarnation of Christ in your cross-cultural worker among a targeted people group. His testimony lives on!

A related, emotionally charged consideration is the expense of a field worker coming home for the funeral of a relative. Do you tell your missionary that you simply can't afford to fly him home to comfort his mother at

"What constitutes an emergency?"

his father's funeral because you weren't prepared? Will you take up a special offering for such an emergency? Do you maintain an emergency fund? What constitutes an emergency?

Carefully think through these and other life-and-death policies.

ATTENDING TO PERSONAL DETAILS

Beyond this array of details that are best handled by the mission agency and/or church leadership under their spiritual and corporate covering, there is a host of logistical matters that can be handled by individuals. The list here merely suggests the innumerable situations that could arise with your particular field worker.

1) Material goods

If their car didn't sell before they left, you could hold

power of attorney to sell it for them—at agreed-upon terms, of course. You could manage the rental or lease of their house or other properties. You could make payments from their bank account for property, insurance or other home-country financial commitments. You could send them the proper income tax forms, absentee ballots for elections, forms for the renewal of licenses, credentials or certificates. You could store their few boxes of personal belongings, which they chose not to sell or take with them. And, of course, you could arrange to send necessary materials to them on time!

One missionary couple sold their car to their dad. When they came home for a summer break, they asked Dad if he had a car they could borrow!

2) Family matters

You may be called upon to be executor of your missionary's will or Living Trust. You may be asked to be the parents of their children if death of both parents should occur. You may be the ideal person to visit or care for their elderly parents. You may be able to provide a home for their college-age child attending school in your town. You may have the contacts to provide the home schooling curriculum materials they need. You may represent your missionary at family gatherings or events. Or, even care for their pet parrot while they are away!

3) Ministry needs

You could gather and mail ministry items to your worker— Bibles, food and clothing for the poor, Sunday school materials and pictures. Many types of technical equipment may be less expensive in the USA or of a better quality. You could become your missionary's source for information about these matters. You could purchase and ship computers, modems, fax machines, hand-crank or solar-powered cassette, CD, DVD or Mp3 players. You might research and expedite purchase of blank CD's, DVDs and other supplies. Or you might put your goers in touch with sources from whom they may purchase directly.

One well-meaning sender secured Mp3 players, for free, that he knew his missionary friend could use. However, the missionary had a local free source for the same item. It is always best to check with your cross-cultural worker before you act.

These jobs only suggest the enormity and diversity of this important support role—the role of a go-fer! Selected members of your sending team with real gifts of service must attend to all your worker's responsibilities that continue in his home country. For, as Paul admonished Timothy, "No man going to war entangles himself with the affairs of daily living" (2 Timothy 2:4). And there is no doubt that your friend is on the front line of spiritual warfare.

A missionary had left her house and cottage in the hands of a couple who assured her of their ability to keep them rented and

"We really do need each other."

maintained. Upon her return from two years in the Middle East, she found the couple had divorced and had sold her antique piano. Her house was trashed and not rented, and the man living in the cottage had not paid rent in six months!

Logistics support is essentially caring for each other in the Body of Christ. The Word teaches a simple doctrine: We really do need each other. We are the Family of God. Paul said that the Body should work together as a whole with all the members having the same care one for another (1 Corinthians 12).

LOGISTICS SUPPORT MEMBERS MUST HAVE CERTAIN QUALIFICATIONS

Diligence: Sometimes it takes a bit of research to find all the correct income tax forms. Sometimes it takes some creative looking to find an inexpensive source or any source for New Testaments in the Uzbek language!

Concern for details: How to mail items—completing the customs forms, packaging, postage, labeling—takes time and communication with the field worker regarding mailing requirements in the host country and detailed concern in working with the US Postal Service or other carrier service.

New missionaries in Peru received a notice from the Lima post office that a package of homemade cookies had arrived from the States. When presented with an exorbitant import duty for the shipment, the missionaries thought they should pay it, for the sake of their relationship with the well-meaning senders ... until an experienced missionary told them the package would have been "accidentally" damaged and all the cookies would be gone anyway! Logistics support must be concerned with details such as import duties on care packages. You don't "inflate" the price of something you are sending to impress them. You may have just increased the cost of them receiving it!

Punctuality: When you get a request for an item from your cross-cultural worker, it is possible that a week or two has already passed since the need became acute. Maybe he thought it could be purchased locally, only to find out that it wasn't available. Finding what was requested, packaging and sending it—in addition to the return mail time—can cause quite a delay. Any procrastination increases the wait.

I just saw a missionary's blog, stating his need for a particular toner cartridge. Hopefully, whoever responds to that request will take the proper number to the store. Also, hopefully, he will not find five or six in his PO box, awaiting import duty!

Sound business practices: Your record keeping and promptness of payment in your missionary's financial dealings is a reflection of *his* integrity in business.

When we went to Peru, we turned the rental management of our house over to a friend. Bills and receipts would accompany every check, he assured us. The records would be kept with accuracy. The businesslike manner of our friend gave us confidence that all would be well when we returned. And it was. On the other hand, when we went to Brazil, a missionary family we knew from Peru moved in, even before we had moved out! "If the roof blows off, be sure to put up a new one," we joked.

Be assured that the peace of mind that you as a logistics support person can provide for a cross-cultural worker is equal in value to the things you do for him. Do you have the gift of administration? Here may be your privileged opportunity to serve as a sender!

FIVE THOUGHTS FROM A LOGISTICS SUPPORT TEAM:

1) Sit down for several sessions with the couple you are sending. Even if they are going out under a well-known mission agency or association, don't presume that all their personal business matters will somehow be taken care of. Go over taxes, past and present. Discuss every financial obligation they have. Find out why they have these bills and why they pay them the way they do and whom to contact when questions arise.

2) Get a full, durable power of attorney for the husband and wife, separately.

3) Set up a record-keeping system with the couple before they leave. Find out how they want their records maintained so that you don't just hand them a stack of old bills and cancelled checks when they return.

4) Make sure that their will or Living Trust is complete and on file with their executor. If that is you, get a safety deposit box. Make sure they have expressed what they want done with their remains. Our missionary, being a very practical guy said, "The cheapest way possible!"

5) Pray about the responsibility you are about to accept. The enemy just loves to confuse and condemn anyone trying to do anything for the Lord—even something as simple (?) as paying a few bills!

IT HAPPENED THIS WAY IN THE CZECH REPUBLIC

The eyes of the Lord run to and fro throughout the whole earth to show Himself strong on behalf of those whose heart is loyal to Him (II Chronicles 16:9). And His eyes rested on a small village church in the Czech Republic. More specifically, He saw willing hearts in a young couple. (We'll call them Ray and Susan.) Their hearts had been moved with compassion for the Bibleless peoples of the world.

(It is one thing to know there is a Bible in your language and you may have to wait for years to have your own copy smuggled into your country. It is yet another—more sad—situation to not have any Scripture in your language or to not even know there is such a thing as the Word of God.)

With this passion in their hearts, Ray and Susan went to their pastor. In prayer, they sensed God's hand in this desire. They joined a Bible translation agency. Along with all that was involved in preparation, the member care director gave them a newly translated copy of *Serving As Senders*. By reading the book, and with the pastor by their side through this new process, they came to realize the importance of developing a relational, personal support team.

However, they were a small village church. Where would they find the number of people to commit to such a long-term agreement as Bible translation requires? In prayer and humility, the pastor and Ray laid aside their doctrinal distinctives and approached the other churches in this village. Openness was expressed by many. A few, though, could not overcome deeply embedded differences.

A meeting time was set. Many came together. They learned about Bible translation. They learned about relational member care. They grasped the seriousness of their commitment, should they agree to it. As meetings continued, a core leadership for each of the areas of support was rising to the challenge. The heart passion of Ray and Susan was being formed in their hearts. The once "only a group of people" was developing into a team. They were uniting around a singular goal—Scripture in the heart language of a yet-to-be-determined people group.

Ray and Susan went to their agency's training. They all waited for the day to know what specific group of the 3000+ peoples would be theirs. Even that anticipation drew them into a greater unity.

One weekend, it was my privilege to be invited to this small village church, to which God had given such a large vision. I shared with the congregation, but my joy was multiplied on that Sunday afternoon. We went to an upstairs room. Gathered together were the pastor, Ray and Susan, and the core leadership drawn from seven denominations! I prayed a silent prayer of thanksgiving: Thank You, Lord, that when peoples' hearts are beating in rhythm with Yours, denominational distinctives do not seem so important.

A vibrant discussion ensued. Questions were being asked and answered. Roles and responsibilities were being clarified. How to work together was becoming clearer. I could sense a true spirit of unity.

And I heard Ray and Susan were sent off well to their first term in a Southeast Asian country.

Lest we leave you, the reader, believing that the principles of this book can easily slip into the working of your church, we must be honest and admit that spiritual warfare becomes more intense in cross-cultural outreach ministry, for both those who go and those who serve as senders. And "things" can go wrong. Such was the case with this church.

It happened that four years later when Ray and Susan were home on their first furlough, my wife and I were again invited to the church. During that four years, spiritual attacks had been launched against the team. One couple had divorced; another key leader had left the church. As we met with them, it was obvious the enemy had scored a heavy blow. Prayer and words of encouragement were offered. More prayer. A clearer understanding of the spiritual assault gave them a stronger determination to regroup and carry on.

To the glory of God and for His Kingdom's sake, Christian workers drawn out from seven churches in a small village tucked in the countryside of the Czech Republic continue to team with Ray and Susan in the ministry of Bible translation.

There is no way of anticipating what your missionary will ask for; there is no knowing when a request will come. Yet one committed to the task and diligent in the work is a rare and prized partner in cross-cultural ministry. You may be just that person.

But for your missionary to sense the full support he needs, other areas of your possible service become important, also. So that he may become "disentangled with the affairs of this life" and preach the Gospel freely, a vital part of the team becomes those who provide the financial support.

(In addition to the individual study below, see the **Group Leader's Guide** for Chapter Three beginning on page 202.)

FOR YOUR PERSONAL INVOLVEMENT

- Read Paul's account of cooperation in the Body of Christ from 1 Corinthians 12. Particularly note the care given to the "less comely" parts.

- In the Book of Acts, underline all references to travel logistics. With today's many communication systems, how could someone "back home" have helped in each of these instances? Ex: Where did Paul and Barnabas sleep that first night back in Antioch?

- Make a list of all the things in your life that would need attention "back home" if you went away for two years. These are probably the things your missionary has to find someone to handle before he leaves.

ACTION STEPS

By the time you have read Chapter Three, completed the *For Your Personal Involvement* section and participated in a group discussion, you should ...

- Understand the potentially vast number of details involved in logistics support.

- Be more aware that we are the Body of Christ and we really do need each other.

- Decide whether God wants you to be on the logistics support team of a cross-cultural worker you know. Check with your church's missions coordinator to see if he knows where you can fit in. Possibly you will have to contact your friend directly and inquire of any logistical need that he may have. Make yourself available to assist in that need.

- Multiply yourself. As you come to understand the value of this type of support, encourage others to consider it as their place in the Body of Christ.

Chapter 4

Financial Support

"It has been a great joy to me that after all this time you have shown such interest in my welfare. I don't mean that you had forgotten me, but up untill now you have had no opportunity of expressing your concern. Nor do I mean that I have been in actual need, for I have learned to be content, whatever the circumstances may be. I know now how to live when things are difficult and I know how to live when things are prosperous."
Philippians 4:10-12

"IN TOTALLY MIRACULOUS ways God opened four major doors to bring us to Cuiaba, Brazil, as Short-Term Assistants (STAs) with Wycliffe.

"Being STAs wasn't new to us. We had spent two eventful years in Peru and thought of serving again—sometime. I had no idea returning to the field was the reason for an appointment at 8 a.m. one September morning with Wycliffe's Superintendent of Children's Education. I thought we were going to talk further about a teacher recruitment program in which I was involved. I had no idea I was the one to be recruited!

"The longer we talked, the more I wondered if God wanted us on the field again—now! By 9:30 a.m., we decided I wasn't the one to go to Nepal; by 10:30 a.m., I had some reservations about Papua New Guinea; by 11:00 a.m., we were praying for God's direction for me to be a principal-teacher in Brazil for a two-year emergency commitment.

"'We're going to Brazil!' I announced as I walked through the front door of our home that day. While my wife, Yvonne, and I prayerfully considered the decision, we knew God would have to open several doors which otherwise could keep us from going.

"The first challenge was regarding our oldest son, Kevin, who was only a semester away from graduation. Would it even be fair to him to change schools again? He had already been in three different high schools! Though we definitely wanted him to go with us, it would have to be his decision. As days merged into weeks, his attitude changed from 'Do your own thing, but don't expect me to go,' to 'Let's get going!'

"Our home represented another obstacle. How could we ever find a family who would be totally responsible for the house for two years? But in God's time schedule He brought close friends to Southern California for a two-year furlough from their ministry with Wycliffe in Peru. They moved in— we moved out, leaving pictures on the walls and linens in the closet!

"A third issue was my mother-in-law's health. She was battling cancer and was really depending on Yvonne for moral support. God took care of her needs through a miraculous healing!

"The fourth door to be opened had dollar signs on it! We learned that the cost of living in Brazil was as high as in Southern California. We sent a letter to our friends—those who we thought would be interested in what we felt sure God wanted us to do. Money began coming in. A bonus on the job. A buyer for the car and travel trailer. Our church board had just decided to double its support for Wycliffe families. Friends pledged toward our monthly needs.

"We received official approval from the Wycliffe Board. Passports and immunizations were now in order. We were assured our visas would arrive between November 12 and 15. We set our departure date: 10 p.m., November 18 from the Los Angeles airport.

"All the normal hectic things were happening: We were trying to buy lightweight clothing in a winter market; packing, weighing, repacking; finding a misplaced birth certificate; sending out another letter; having the last gala round of visits with friends.

"Then November 18 came. At 8 a.m. I was making the final tally of our financial situation—a task I had intentionally delayed. I just couldn't make it all add up. We were $50 a month short.

"'I just cannot sign our Statement of Financial Preparedness,' I regretfully told Yvonne and our friends. We all laughed at the ridiculousness of our situation. Luggage filled the living room. The kids were checked out of school. Our car was sold. Our friends were already living with us—and wanted us to get out of *their* house! All good-byes had been said. We were holding thousands of dollars of non-fundable airline tickets in our hands. We'd radioed Brazil that we were on our way. And here we were, $50 a month short of our financial support goal!

"'The Lord must be planning to send in some money today,' I said as I put the statement aside, unsigned.

"At 9 a.m. Yvonne's mother called, asking if we needed any money. She then related an incredible story about Myrna, a woman in my father-in-law's church. She had been on our financial support team during our time with Wycliffe in Peru, and she had heard us present the financial needs for this new venture in Brazil. Unknown to us, she had been struggling for several weeks for a way in which God could use her again on our financial support team.

"But it was now the night before we were to leave. Myrna spent a sleepless vigil asking the Lord for some way that she could still help us. Their business was in financial difficulties and their house had just been robbed. At 4 a.m. she dozed off and at 7 a.m. was up preparing to go to a church missions meeting. At 8 a.m. (while I was doing my figuring) she put on a coat she hadn't worn since the previous winter. She put her hand in the pocket and, to her amazement, drew out $1,200 in cash! The thief who had stolen two of her husband's suits in that closet three nights before had completely missed the treasure in her coat!

"'This is for the Pirolos!' she shouted. 'Thank you, Lord, for Your faithfulness!'

"And I said, 'Praise the Lord!' The $1,200 she found in the pocket and wanted us to have was exactly the $50 support for 24 months that we lacked. I ran for the Statement of Financial Preparedness and signed, 'Yes, we are ready to go!'"

Financial support is the most controversial, thus the most talked-about of the six areas of support. In fact, when you mention missionary support, most people think of nothing else but money.

We walk through the marketplaces of the Christian world, confronted by a spectrum of contradictions. On the one hand, we see the bloated stomachs and are made to feel guilty by the millions who are starving to death because we do not give $38 to such-and-such an organization. At the other extreme, we are told, "Prosperity is your divine right!" Where do we turn for balance in financial responsibility?

To further complicate the issue is the problem that a god of this age in America is materialism. The United States, represents less than 5% of the world's population, yet consumes 20% of the earth's manufactured goods and 60% of all petroleum products. In addition, the media creates, then preys upon society's poor self-image by saying, "You aren't good enough ... until you use our product!" So we endlessly toil to purchase this and that, only to find out in next week's commercial that a "new and improved" version is now available. As the bumper sticker says, "I owe, I owe, so off to work I go!" How do we rise above the trivia of this world to see financial responsibility from God's perspective?

His Word, of course, communicates His perspective. On the stub of every pay check received by Christians could be the words of Deuteronomy 8:18: "Remember the Lord your God, for it is He who gives you the ability to produce wealth." God is the owner of—everything; we are simply His stewards. When we look at that paycheck and think, "This is mine," we err. We should be thinking about how the Owner of it wants us to use it.

More than seven out of every ten dollars held by Christians in the world are in the hands of American Christians! As we hold this wealth, then, we must ask the next question: "Why has God so blessed His people in America?" Again, the Word gives a clear answer: "God be merciful to us and bless us and cause Your face to shine upon us *so that* Your way may be known on earth and Your salvation among all nations" (Psalm 67:1-2). God's principle that His people are blessed to be a blessing was established in the covenant He made with Abraham (Genesis 12).

> "God bless us *so that* His salvation may be known among all nations."

Some of the more familiar methods of securing finances to bless the world through cross-cultural outreach ministry include bake sales and car washes, pancake breakfasts and cardboard, bottle and can recycling. And in an increasingly waste-conscious economy, these endeavors do generate some working capital. A neighborhood yard sale with all or a portion of the proceeds going to a missions project or missionary can bring families together for good causes. Arts and crafts items can be made and sold and again the profit given to a missionary. An organization has an annual golf tournament to generate income. God blesses us with ingenuity, mouth-watering recipes and entrepreneurial skills so that we can financially bless the spread of His Kingdom.

However, the time will come when your cross-cultural outreach ministry has grown beyond the funds that can be generated by these methods. Now diligent effort must be made to look beyond these endeavors to some more fundamental, long-lasting ways of securing finances for cross-cultural outreach ministry. Let's look at three areas of Biblical stewardship: giving, lifestyle and managing wealth.

GIVING

We know the Word: God loves a cheerful giver; It is more blessed to give than to receive; Give, and it shall be given unto you; When you give. ... Yet the brilliance of the Bible's simple teaching on the principle of giving invariably gets around to "how much" which inevitably leads to tithing which ultimately deals with the nitty-gritty of "Do I tithe on my net or on my gross?" And we have run into the same dead end the Jews faced when Jesus said to them: "You pay tithe of mint and dill and cummin, but omit the weightier matters of the Law. ... You strain out the gnat and swallow the camel" (Matthew 23:23-24)!

The discipline of tithing (which Jesus commended the Jews for doing) leads a Christian to a deeper commitment of "generous, cheerful, hilarious" giving (2 Corinthians 9:7), which grows into the willing mind principle of 2 Corinthians 8:12-14: "That there may be an equality!"

Using this principle, as long as we compare ourselves only to those wealthier than we are, we don't feel too compelled to give. When we enlarge our vision to encompass the world, however, the principle of equality has us giving and giving some more since the poverty level in America is in the top 4-5% of world family income. We are indeed rich in finances. A simple Google search for sites such as www.100people.org will yield statistics to give you perspective on comparative wealth. For example, if you keep your food in a refrigerator, clothes in a closet, have a roof over your head and a bed to sleep in, you are richer than 75% of the entire world population.

A hymn of the Church says: "I surrender all. I surrender all. All to Jesus I surrender; I surrender all." May we, in our responsible stewardship of finances, grapple with God's Word and the work of the Holy Spirit in our lives to that point of full surrender. Certainly God allows us to spend what is necessary for our living expenses. We have unrestricted choice in determining that amount. In full surrender, what will we do with the excess? That is the point of decision.

Before we go on, let's back up to the basic concept of tithing: If every Christian in your fellowship tithed, just that tithe would keep the finance committee busy meeting every week to determine its disbursement! We must recognize, however, that a "tithe" means 10%. As we moved into the 21st Century, statistics said that all charitable giving amounted to 1.7%! Though there has been an increase, it remains quite static at 2.2%!

The issues that surround tithing are not limited to wealthy nations. I was in the backcountry of a large nation. The subject of tithing came up. Their "excuse" for not tithing was that they don't use money a lot. They barter. One grows corn; another hogs. A hog is worth a certain number of bushels of corn. I asked if they all had chickens? Yes. Do they lay eggs? Yes. Then, one egg goes to the pastor and you get to keep nine!

None of us likes to hear a 20-minute sermon on giving before the offering is taken. But the very concept of "taking" an offering instead of "freely you have received, freely give" (Matthew 10:8) might be educating us to be miserly in our giving. Sometimes even the prayer said before the offering does more to support our meager giving than encourage a "generous, hilarious" freewill gift: "Father, You know we only have these few pennies to give to You. But we know that You will multiply them so the whole world can believe in You!" And we put our wallets away and pull out our loose change—if we have any!

Or we are taught to "pay" our tithes. As with any other bill, therefore, a conscious or unconscious resentment can develop. Rather, the Bible urges that God's people "bring all the tithes into the storehouse" (Malachi 3:10). "Lay up for yourselves treasures in Heaven, where moth and rust don't corrupt" (Matthew 6:20). That sounds more like securing a sound investment than "paying a bill." And that grows into, "What a privilege that God would allow me to be a part of His Plan of the Ages. He could get along without my money, for "He owns the cattle on a thousand hills" (Psalm 50:10). But the Lord is giving me an opportunity to invest in His Kingdom!" And *I'll reap the benefits!*

Giving is an act of intelligent worship. "Let every man who will do it willingly from his heart bring Me an offering" (Exodus 25:2). "Every man shall give as he is able" (Deuteronomy 16:17). "Every man according to his ability determined to send relief" (Acts 11:29). "But first there must be a willing mind" (2 Corinthians 8:12). "Let every one give as he has purposed in his heart" (2 Corinthians 9:7).

> "Giving is an act of intelligent worship."

What do we learn from God's Word? That generous, cheerful, hilarious giving is not an awkward interruption to worship, but the very essence of it. (Listen to a church's "family counsel" meeting: *A Heart Made Willing* available at ERI's ACTS Media Library: www.eri.org. Also, read Randy Alcorn's excellent book, *The Treasure Principle*, available at www.epm.org.)

HOW CAN WE BE WISE ABOUT OUR GIVING?

Unfortunately, not all individuals and organizations vying for your support dollars are themselves wise stewards. There are three questions you must ask to verify their accountability:

1) *Is the money you give going for what they say it is? Do they take 60 cents of your dollar to raise additional funds?* A dedicated sender once gave $30,000 to an international project. A year later, the ones who had solicited this gift came back to him, apologizing that they had not used the money as they had told him. Would he forgive them? Did he want his money back? An apology doesn't happen often! More likely the funds are hidden in the language of the bookkeeper's report! An alarming statistic gives us caution: More money is embezzled by 'Christian' leaders each year than is given to missions.

2) *Is the project or missionary service really hitting a decisive point of battle for souls?* God wants us to be a part of ministries that yield "fruit that remains."

You might even have to say "no" to your closest friend's appeal if you sense his summer of service sounds more like a surf and sun holiday or if he is going to do what the nationals could or would do!

Worthwhile missionary service is as diverse as the creative genius of God flowing through His obedient servants. And some of the activities seem way out there—somewhere! But if they are really hitting a decisive point of battle for the souls of mankind, there will be a line of correlation that can be traced to "fruit that remains." Remember, a *decisive point* answers two questions in the affirmative: Is it worth doing? Do we have the resources to do it?

One of my wife's jobs in Peru was keeping track of the airplane radio parts. Being a "people-person", that could have been a hard task to do! How could that be related to the salvation of the tribal people of Peru? Well, radio parts are needed to keep the radios functioning *so that* the airplanes can fly *so that* the translators can get to their villages *so that* they can translate the Scripture into the heart languages of the people *so that* they can read the Word *so that* they can trust in Christ as Savior! Whew! Counting radio parts...a long way from the salvation of the lost, but with a direct line of correlation. Thus, it *was* a decisive point of battle.

3) *If your cross-cultural worker is going out through a US-based organization, what is the US administrative/field use ratio of the mission's funds?* That is, how much is spent in the States to get one dollar to the field? Is it under 15%? Are the US personnel living on a comparable level to their field workers? How do they secure their finances? (By the way, if an organization doesn't want to answer this type of question, you already have a pretty good idea of their

accountability!) A list of appropriate questions to ask is available at www.davidmays.org/agencypartner.pdf. Better still, ask David for his *Stuff CD*—500 pages of good "stuff" to know about missions. (www.davidmays.org)

God owns all, yet He is the most frugal economist! He wastes nothing. Twelve baskets full picked up; seven baskets full picked up (Mark 8:19-20). Need we say more?

Yet, may a missionary spend the "Lord's money" on an ice cream cone? One friend confessed that he and his family were walking down a street (back home), having just come out of Baskin Robbins, each enjoying an ice cream cone. Then, down the street, he saw a member from his supporting church. They all quickly dashed into an alley so as not to be seen!

LIFESTYLE

Statistics can bore or shock or motivate. For example: Americans spend as much on chewing gum in a year as they give to missions. Americans pay as much for pet food in 52 days as they invest annually on missions. On one day, February 14, Americans spend more money to say, "I love you" with Valentines Day cards than that which is spent in the whole month of February (and each of the other months) to tell a lost and dying world that God loves them! Does our lifestyle, as Jesus said, tell us where our heart is (Luke 12:13-34)?

(In this chapter, and throughout the book, we quote numerous statistics and details that change with time. The Internet has become the "source of choice" for finding— everything! Where specific websites or emails are not given or stats seem unbelievable, a Google search will easily direct you to "1.3 million results in 0.13 seconds!")

The *Queen Mary*, a huge cruise ship, was designed and built as a luxury vessel; yet during World War II it was converted to serve as a troop carrier. Today the museum aboard the *Queen Mary* affords a stunning contrast between the lifestyles appropriate in peace and war. On one side of a partition, the tables prepared for high society hold a dazzling array of china, crystal and silver. On the other side, one metal tray with indentations replaces 15 dishes and saucers. Bunks, four tiers high, accommodate 15,000 troops in contrast to the 3,000 wealthy patrons in peacetime transport. (Each bunk slept two soldiers; they slept in shifts.) To so drastically reconstruct the vessel took a national emergency. The survival of a nation depended upon it. Should you replace your china with metal trays? No! But allow the Holy Spirit to challenge every aspect of your lifestyle.

Our Master calls out, "Rescue the perishing!" The Captain of the Lord of Hosts has trumpeted a clear sound for battle. But the cry of the perishing is often lost in the din of self-survival. While pursuing comfort we can easily ignore Christ's warning in Scripture, "He who would seek to save his life will lose it" (Luke 17:33). We decry the diseases of the underdeveloped nations: tuberculosis, malnutrition, parasites, typhoid and others. Yet America has virtually invented a whole new set of affluence-related diseases: obesity, arteriosclerosis, heart disease, strokes, lung cancer, cirrhosis of the liver and more. In "saving" ourselves we are well on our way to losing ourselves!

Any good cross-cultural training teaches the missionary to adapt as much as possible to the lifestyle of those he is going to minister among—a simpler lifestyle, a lowered consumption of goods, a make-do and/or seek-a-creative-alternative attitude. This forms a solid principle of bonding—establishing a sense of belonging with the ones he serves.

Those who serve as senders might experience a new sense of belonging and vision of their part in rescuing the perishing if they, too, would adopt a lifestyle that approximates that of those they are sending. Senders who take on this challenge often find that somehow their quality of life measurably improves.

A diligent financial support team member must allow the radical challenges of these statements to question his lifestyle:

1) If my lifestyle runs out of money before the month runs out of days, a humbling but good starting point might be for me to ask for help in personal financial management.

2) If my lifestyle looks into a five-foot-long closet of clothes and doesn't see "a thing to wear," possibly a new reading of "Do not be anxious about what clothes you will put on, for the body is more than clothing" (Luke 12:22-23) might give me a new perspective on the situation.

3) If my lifestyle demands a status symbol for transportation (or possession of anything for the purpose of making others envious), I should check carefully Christ's parable regarding taking the seat of honor in Luke 14:7-14.

4) If my lifestyle builds long hallways and huge bedrooms and bathrooms for each family member and a living room, family room, recreation room and parlor, it might be well for me to consider my Christian longings for a home in the city "whose builder and maker is God" (Hebrews 11:10).

5) If my lifestyle careens on the roller coasters of thrills and frills of continual entertainment, it might be well for me to reduce the speed and turn down the volume enough to notice that life is ready to give free excitement and exhilaration through natural beauty (Psalm 19:1-3), fellowship (Acts 2:42) and worship (Psalm 34:1-4).

Do not allow the enemy to bring condemnation from any of those statements, but prayerfully consider the Holy Spirit's dealing in your life and yield to His will. For "He who has begun a good work in you will bring it to completion." This is Paul's encouragement to those who were partnering with him in cross-cultural ministry. (Read Philippians 1:5-6; also Philippians 2:12 and 13.)

God's direction regarding finances is not one-size-fits-all. There is no hint that Jesus ever told Mary, Martha and Lazarus to sell any of their wealth. And the record suggests they were quite well to do! Yet to the rich young ruler, He said, "Sell all" (Matthew 19:21). He who dies with the most toys—still dies! As Randy Alcorn says in his book, *The Treasure Principle*, "You can't take it with you—but you *can* send it on ahead." Laying up treasure in Heaven is the Biblical wording (Matthew 6:20).

Although many books on the subject of Christian finance only make us feel guilty or tell us to tighten our belts, an excellent book on this subject is by Doris Janzen Longacre. *Living More With Less* contains literally hundreds of practical lifestyle changes that encompass every aspect of finance. And it assures you of an enhanced way of life.

> ## "Living more with less could enhance your lifestyle!"

Christians with a renewed lifestyle can free up thousands—even millions—of creative dollars for cross-cultural ministry. Living more with less is an exciting, viable option.

MANAGING WEALTH

No more than a cursory glance at the parable of the talents (Matthew 25:14-30) assures us that the Lord expects us to be wise in managing the wealth He has entrusted to us. In a related parable in Luke 19:11-27, He tells us to "occupy—be about My work in a businesslike manner—until I come."

We can exercise Christian stewardship on two levels: financial practices on the field and financial resources behind the lines.

Financial Practices On The Battlefield

- Missionaries could implement plans that include short-term—two-four year—assignments instead of strategies that demand costly real estate or other long-term investment. Admittedly, some cross-cultural assignments require a very long commitment—Bible translation, for one. But many mission assignments could be turned over to nationals sooner than they are so that your missionary could move on to new areas of need. A sad but valid criticism is that many jobs still being done by missionaries could be handled more effectively by nationals! Notice Paul's strong encouragement to Titus to "appoint elders in every city" (Titus 1:5). His further note, quoting Crete's own poet, suggests Titus was having a hard time finding qualified men—but he was still to get on with it (Titus 1:12)!

• Another practice of Biblical times was to move (for one reason or another) to a new area, become a resident of that country and seek employment. (Read Acts 18:1-19 for the example of Aquila and Priscilla.) In some situations your missionary could do this and release his funds for others.

• Making a greater use of tentmaker opportunities gets your missionary living and working with the people. Teaching English as a second language is one of the best opportunities; becoming an international student is a close second. Beyond these are thousands of jobs around the world that would allow your missionary to get *Out of the Saltshaker and Into the World* as a book by Rebecca Pippert challenges. There are some serious considerations, however, that must be given to this type of ministry. Don Hamilton's book *Tentmakers Speak* is particularly helpful reading in this area. A Google search of 'Business As Mission' yielded 45,100,000 results in 0.22 seconds! Business As Mission (BAM) has become a 21st Century thrust in sharing Christ through business.

Google search "expatriate workers" to read about the nine million workers just in Saudi Arabia. Several agencies in the Philippines train Christian workers in how to witness in their adopted country. Filipino workers in Saudi Arabia are facing great persecution, but that has only emboldened them to a greater word of testimony.

• Self-support by independently wealthy or retired people is becoming a more viable option. With our increasing senior citizen population, agencies are specifically recruiting these people. The Finisher's Project is leading the way in this endeavor to challenge early retirees to give the second half of their adult life to cross-cultural ministry service (www.finishers.org).

- Living *among* the people instead of in guarded, gated communities in the suburbs may free needed funds. Perhaps even a team house right in the community of the targeted people would be wise. One time we were visiting missionary friends in Hong Kong. After a meal in their cramped seventh floor flat (apartment), Dennis took me out on the small balcony. He pushed the drying clothes aside and said, "There it is, Neal. 'Missionary Hill'.

> "Living *among* the people follows the example of Jesus and Paul."

Behind those walls, topped with razor barbed wire are all the 'goodies' the missionaries have brought from home. The vapor lights and Doberman dogs give further protection. They do venture out once in a while to minister."

Paul reminded the elders of Ephesus, "You know how ever since I first came to Asia, how I have lived among you" (Acts 20:18). About Jesus, John wrote, "The Word was made flesh and dwelt among us" (John 1:14). Jesus was a powerful example of living with the people. Later He said, "In the same way My Father sent Me, I am now sending you" (John 20:21).

- The greater use of non-Western workers and methods is a fast-growing trend as God has sovereignly raised up a "new wave" of missionary thrust. It is coming from Eastern and Southern Hemisphere nations. Missionaries from America can work with this move of God! "Fruit that remains" is our goal. How can we most effectively cooperate with this Divine Plan? Paul, that great missionary statesman of the first century serves as an excellent model—again!

He was an evangelist. Most often we read of his preaching the Gospel. There were only a few exceptions—the most notable being his several years of teaching in Ephesus. However, he did have a team of teachers (Timothy and Titus are the best known, but there were many others— see Acts 20:4) who were left behind to find faithful men— nationals—and teach them the Word in such a way that they would go out to teach others (2 Timothy 2:2).

Our tendency to think our ways are the best in the world has created a rather distorted picture of other cultures. We do need to remember that they are different, not inferior. Nationals trained in solid teaching of the Word are then better able to communicate to their own culture than a foreign missionary.

A pastor went to another country and culture to "plant a church." With American money and regular support teams from home, he had a good measure of success. He was also mentoring a national to become the pastor. After a time, he turned the church over to the national and left. All was well to this point. Several years later, he returned to visit. To his dismay, the church no longer "looked" like the one he had planted. It had taken on local cultural characteristics. He demoted the national pastor and resumed the position himself!

If you are in a position to formulate policy or financially support missionaries, be a wise and faithful steward. Study and network with mission strategists about wise financial policies. Don't establish a ministry that must forever be subsidized by Western money after being turned over to nationals. Don't teach nationals discipling methods that require anything not easily accessible in their culture— big buildings or perhaps any buildings, expensive books, sound systems, video equipment, vehicles, etc. Do let the simplicity of the Gospel be clothed in the nationals' own cultural garb.

I was recently talking with a missionary on home
assignment. He was almost apologetic in describing the
simple structure the missionaries had helped the nationals
build for their place of meeting. He was used to defending
his work to the Western mind that expects lavish church
buildings! On the contrary, in my mind, I was rejoicing! If
they want to receive the offering in a cowboy boot placed
by the door, who am I to say, "No! No! Do it this way?"

There are additional ways of saving missionary dollars.
They are found in how we manage His wealth entrusted to
us back home.

Financial Resources Behind The Lines

- *Cooperatives.* A Christian co-op could offer extensive
  possibilities to manage the wealth God has given us.
  Whether in the area of food or clothing, household items
  or services; whether community sized, within a church or
  in a neighborhood, a Christian co-op is an excellent way
  to free up finances for the advancement of the Kingdom.

- *Thrift stores.* In the first century, Christians had "all things
  in common" (Acts 4:32). Today we can share our excess
  goods by letting others buy them through a thrift store.
  It could be totally supplied by free goods and operated
  by volunteers. Probably one paid manager to keep it
  operating smoothly would be good. Well-managed, this
  type of business could give its proceeds to missions.

  One ministry funds the work of two orphanages through
  a network of three thrift stores. There are, of course,
  government regulations. And it would require diligent
  business practices, but the rewards of funding more field
  workers or study Bibles for national pastors or church-
  planting teams is well worth the energy.

- *Multi-level sales.* These businesses continue to capture the
  market of distribution of certain goods and services (as well

as a lot of criticism). Therefore, in choosing a company, it is essential to identify with one that is selling a marketable product and one whose quality and cost is competitive with traditional marketing. Some organizations will allow an entire non-profit group to enter the "down line."

- *Mutual fund investing.* It is not known just what markets the stewards traded in in the parable of the talents, but it is impossible that they just "put it in the bank." The master would have had to be gone on a very long journey to double the money even at 10% interest. And the unfaithful steward was reprimanded for not at least putting it in the bank (Matthew 25:14-30). You probably know or know those who know how to bring the surpluses of your church friends' liquid assets together in mutual fund investing. This requires very careful agreed-upon security measures and other details that need to be worked out, but one $100,000 investment might very well yield a greater rate of interest than ten $10,000 investments.

- *Estate planning.* This source of funds holds good, long-term money available for Kingdom work. Unfortunately, it is a method already being abused by some Christian organizations. Nonetheless, it is an area in which we have been called upon to be faithful stewards.

  > "An experienced financial manager could help with strategic investments."

  Millions of dollars per year go into state coffers because about 55% of our population dies without a will! This area does require a knowledgeable consultant, but generating mission funds through estate planning can be done in good taste, and for His glory.

- *Grant funding.* Another source of money for warfare against the enemy lies in the estates of certain philanthropic individuals and societies. Yes, it is a lot of work to write the proposals. Yes, many more will say no than yes, but literally millions of dollars are available for the right group doing the right thing and having written the right proposal.

- *Matching funds.* It is an accepted and growing practice of industry and individuals to "match funds" for worthy causes. This has been employed mostly in gifts to educational institutions. However, the tax benefit to the company is the same whether to one non-profit organization or another. It would probably work best to name some specific project in your ministry country.

  Do you know a retired banker or other financial manager whose dealings with money are keen with years of experience? Nudge him to put those skills to the Master's use in managing these types of financial resources. Maybe *you* are that person!

- *Income tax.* Some people claim "no deductions," allowing the government to use their money all year interest free just so they can use the "forced savings" in their refund. How much better would be the disciplined saving of that amount—at least at bank rates! At the end of the year (or quarter), pay the government its due and give the interest earned to your cross-cultural worker's support fund. Too little an amount? Remember the widow's two mites (Luke 21:2).

- *Equity.* If you have owned real property for some years, the equity could be put out at interest to generate dollars for cross-cultural ministry. An equity line of credit can be obtained at a low interest rate. With that sum of money, it is not difficult to find an investment at a safe, but higher rate. That's exactly what a bank does with your savings account!

However, get sound financial counsel about any of these suggestions from trustworthy people who understand money well and have a good track record themselves. Also, there are journals you can study. And there is the Holy Spirit to guide your bold actions to free up creative dollars for cross-cultural outreach ministry.

World economic crises are daily in our news: OPEC nations at a conference table in the Middle East affect gasoline prices in the West. High consumption nations import cheap products from economically impoverished countries, while sending back ever-higher-priced manufactured goods. International companies buy land to produce export crops, forcing local people to pay higher prices on imported food. Producers dump a million tons of grain in the ocean to maintain marketable prices.

On a scale far greater than we can comprehend, many Christians ignorantly or glibly contribute to the economic injustice of the world, shrugging off any responsibility with a simple "What can one person do?" God's response is in the singular: "But whoever has the world's goods and sees his brother in need, and hardens his heart against him, how does the love of God abide in him" (1 John 3:17)? Or, for even stronger words from our Lord, read Proverbs 24:11-12!

In all of the areas we have considered, the influence of one person is small. But it is one by one that we will stand before Him and give an accounting of our actions: Will it be "wood, hay, stubble" or "gold, silver and precious stones" (1 Corinthians 3:12-13)?

We are to become "faithful ... in the unrighteous riches" so that the Lord will "commit to our trust the true riches" (Luke 16:1-12).

It is Happening This Way in Sri Lanka

Just a small island nation. But with two major languages: Tamil and Sinhala. An email from the Lanka Bible School, Publications Division requested being able to translate *Serving As Senders* into those two languages. How surprised I was to know that this nation would want to learn how to care for missionaries they send out. Rather, how surprised I was that Sri Lanka was sending out missionaries!

It was my privilege to be there for the dedication of the translations. Now, many years later comes this story:

> *Serving As Senders* has been an invaluable tool for training our overseas workers in Sri Lanka. Yes, unfortunately, sending countries are still letting people go without a good sending church and team. So, when they arrive here, it is my responsibility as the Member Care Chairperson to help them develop a partnership team. It is quite a bit more difficult for them to do long distance, but with the help of the book (and our insistence), it can be done.
>
> But a far greater joy is to be able to regularly consult the Tamil or Sinhala translation. We use them to train those who are stepping out from Sri Lanka to challenging places in Southeast Asia, as well as those who are learning how to be "senders" from Sri Lanka. Each session awakens both the senders and missionaries to the realities of the upcoming challenges, and it guides our missionaries as they develop a supportive home base. It is a real educational process, again, both for the missionaries and for the team they develop. To make such a commitment to a friend who is leaving them is not a common practice in our culture. It has been a tremendous gift to have the book available here. It is thorough and full of such practical materials.

It is Happening This Way in the Middle East

(For security reasons, names and countries are omitted. The following was submitted by the director of a mission agency.)

> I am grateful to God to have found this book many years ago. As I read it, I realized the importance of these principles for our missionaries and our churches. Our organization has distributed the book to church leaders in the different Arab countries. It is obviously a resource the churches need to learn how to care for the missionaries they are sending out.

I have received many comments of appreciation. They fall into three general categories:

1) "The subject of the book is unique. There aren't any other books like it in Arabic." This statement by itself may not sound like much, but it tells me that they are greatly appreciating this resource. I am sure they are giving serious thought to its importance in their work as pastors sending out missionaries. It is not easy to consider a new concept. For some pastors, it will take a bit of time to figure out how to apply these principles to their specific situation.

2) "Implementing the topic of the book is a great blessing for the many missionaries working in different fields outside their own country." I rejoice with these missionaries who applied the six principles of member care in developing their support team as they prepared to go to another country. I only pray that with these concepts so new, that those who committed to be involved will fulfill their commitment.

3) "The book has opened our church's eyes to their responsibility toward the mission fields and our missionaries." Statements like this have been the greatest joy to me. As the director of a mission agency, it is a great relief to hear that churches are taking a more active role in the missionary endeavor. We, as an agency, had carried the load for too long. That is why, when I first read this book, I knew it was for us to use. It needed to be translated into Arabic. There is rejoicing in Heaven also, I believe, as churches are partnering with us in the area of member care.

What a blessing it is when people give of their substance so that His Good News can go forth. But there is more to the full measure of support needed by your cross-cultural worker. The nickname given to James (the brother of our Lord) was "camel-knees" from all the time he spent in prayer. Consider the concert of prayer support you can offer to God on behalf of your worker.

(In addition to the individual study below, see the **Group Leader's Guide** for Chapter Four beginning on page 204.)

FOR YOUR PERSONAL INVOLVEMENT

• Paul had quite a bit to say about his financial support (or lack thereof)! Read each of the following passages and try to determine Paul's philosophy regarding financial support: 1 Corinthians 9; 2 Corinthians 12:13-19; Philippians 4:10-19; Philemon 18-22.

• Do an Old and New Testament word study on tithing. Discover that it is a principle of God's Kingdom that works! Include Abraham's refusal to receive money from the king of Sodom, yet he himself gave a tithe to Melchizedek, King of Salem (Genesis 14; Hebrews 7:1-2). This was instituted before the Mosaic or Levitical Law.

• Do an Old and New Testament word study of the "willing mind" principle. Note how often this or a similar phrase is associated with financial giving. Begin with Exodus 25. Go to 1 Chronicles 29. There are many more, but be sure to include 2 Corinthians 8:12-14.

• Without changing your spending patterns, for one month keep a detailed record of every expenditure you make. Then prayerfully begin listing areas in your lifestyle where there might possibly be unnecessary expenditures. Use the five statements on page 81 to challenge you in this activity.

• Name several commercial jingle phrases that if followed could easily distract you from giving financial support to your missionary. Ex: "Shop 'til you drop!" Determine how you are going to combat the impact of materialism in your life.

Action Steps

By the time you have read Chapter Four, completed the *For Your Personal Involvement* section and participated in a group discussion, you should ...

- Purchase Randy Alcorn's book, *The Treasure Principle*. Life-transforming!

- Purchase Doris Longacre's book, *Living More With Less*. Hundreds of practical ideas!

- Plan to attend a Christian financial management seminar in your area.

- Prepare a will or Living Trust.

- Know if you are to be a part of a missionary's financial support team. If yes, let him know of your commitment. Find out where and how to send your check. Let him know the amount the Lord has put on your heart.

- Multiply yourself. Look for others who have their finances in order and wish to see their funds used for Kingdom work.

CHAPTER 5

Prayer Support

*"Praying always with all prayer and supplication
in the Spirit."*
Ephesians 6:18a

I N 1923 HELEN MOLLENKOF, a young teenager, attended
a Keswick Conference in New Jersey. The speaker was L.
L. Legters, who along with Cameron Townsend many years
later would found Wycliffe Bible Translators.

God had given Legters a deep burden for all the indigenous
people of Mexico and Central America who had no Bible in
their own language. Speaking at the Keswick Conference, he
challenged the young people to take the name of one language
group in Mexico and pray for that people—that God would open
the doors so His Word could be translated into the language of
their heart.

Helen was one of those who answered the challenge. She
stepped forward and picked the name of a people she'd never
heard of before: the Mazahua. She wrote the name on the flyleaf
of her Bible. Then, closing her eyes, this teen-aged girl promised
the Lord she would pray for them until they had the Bible
translated into their own language.

Helen went ahead with life. She graduated from school,
became a nurse and joined the Women's Union Missionary

Society. She was then sent to India, where she served as a missionary for the next thirty-five years. One of her ongoing prayer concerns was for the Mazahua people.

In 1967 Helen returned to the States to retire in Lancaster, Pennsylvania. Some time later, for some unexplained reason, she felt free to stop praying for the Mazahua people.

In 1981 she picked up her local newspaper and read an interview with Pat Hamric who, like herself, was a long-term missionary. As she read she discovered to her amazement that Pat, along with Hazel Spotts and Don and Shirley Stewart, had been Bible translators among the Mazahua people.

Overjoyed, she found Pat's address and wrote to her: "I think you might be interested in my contact with the Mazahua Indians through prayer."

She told Pat about the Keswick meeting, how L. L. Letgers had challenged them to take the name of one language group in Mexico, and her commitment to pray.

Pat replied, "The New Testament is complete. It was dedicated in January of 1970!"

Helen realized that January 1970 was the very time the Lord lifted her burden to pray!

In 1972, a woman opened her World Atlas to the Middle East and began praying for a city not far from Tehran, Iran. Through the years there were other prayers, for sure. Always on her heart, however, was the spiritual welfare of this city. Years later, a national from that county came to her church in America. After the service, she dashed over to him. "Where are you from in Iran?" she asked.

He replied, "You won't have heard of it; it is an insignificant city," but he shared the name of the town.

"I've been praying for that city for 34 years!" she blurted out through tears of joy.

"Thirty-four years?" the Iranian brother asked incredulously. "I got saved 34 years ago. I now lead 400 believers in the city."

What powerful testimonies of the significance of prayer in God's global plan! A plethora of articles and books abound on the topic of prayer. A Google search will yield an endless list. What is the sum of their message? The words of Augustine may summarize, "Without God, we cannot; but without us, God will not."

In His sovereignty, God has voluntarily linked Himself to human cooperation. He has inextricably bound Himself to the prayer of faith of His children. He merges His working with man's praying.

Though this is a deep mystery, it is clearly revealed in the Word and throughout history. Joshua's day in battle would have gone poorly without Moses' prayer (Exodus 17). Jacob's place in Israel's history would not have been the same without Penuel (Genesis 32). The cross would have been intolerable without Gethsemane (Luke 22).

Today one can stand in the bedroom where John Wesley and the members of the "Holy Club" held their prayer meetings, a force God used to ignite a revival that was felt around the world.

Consider Evan Roberts and his friends prostrating themselves before the Lord night after night, resulting in the Welsh Revival. Consider the Prayer Mountain in Seoul, Korea, which gave impetus to the growth of several of the largest churches in the world. And the revival that swept Brazil was evidenced by extra police being put on duty to control traffic in several major cities on prayer meeting night! Following that revival, the Church in Brazil is now a leading missionary sending force.

Prayer initiatives of each succeeding generation point to the vitality of intercession. In no greater arena of human activity is this mysterious union of our prayer and God's work seen than in the mission of the Church.

Jesus was going about all the cities and villages, teaching in their synagogues and preaching the Gospel of the Kingdom, but when He saw the multitudes, He was moved with compassion. Then He said to His disciples, "The harvest is great, but the laborers are few. Therefore, pray to the Lord of the harvest to send forth laborers into His harvest." Three verses later, He sent them out two by two (Matthew 9-10)!

At the end of time, Christ the Lamb will be extolled: "You were slain and have redeemed us to God by Your blood out of every kindred and tongue and people and nation" (Revelation 5:9). The twenty-four elders singing this new song will be holding golden vials full of incense, which are the *prayers of saints* (Revelations 5:8)! Some of those are the prayers you are praying for your missionary!

Paul in his masterful Ephesians 6 discourse on spiritual warfare not only clearly described the armor for our protection in war, but also identified two of the major weapons of our warfare: the Sword of the Spirit and spiritual prayers. His urgency was

> "The vials of incense before His throne are *your* prayers!"

expressed: "*Praying always with all prayers and supplication in the Spirit.*"

As a missionary of the first century, he was continually calling on the churches for prayer support: "Brethren, pray for us" he simply stated in 1 and 2 Thessalonians and Hebrews. His appeal to the Christians in Rome seemed a bit more pressing: "I beseech you, brethren ... that you *strive* together with me in your prayers to God for me" (Romans 15:30). Paul assumed Philemon was on his prayer support team (Philemon 22). To the church in Philippi, he stated his confidence that what he was experiencing would turn out for the good of his soul because of their prayers and the resources of the Spirit of Jesus Christ (Philippians 1:19)—bringing us back to that insoluble cooperation of God and man in prayer.

In spite of all of her lamentable weaknesses, appalling failures and indefensible shortcomings, the Church is the mightiest—the only—force that is contesting satan's rule in human affairs! And that Church on her knees is the purifying and preserving influence which has kept the fabric of all we call civilization from total disintegration, decay and despair.

Samuel Chadwick said, "The one concern of the devil is to keep Christians from praying. He fears nothing from prayerless studies, prayerless works and prayerless religion. He laughs at our toil, mocks at our wisdom, but trembles when we pray!"

Prayer is not begging God to do something He is loath to do. It is not overcoming God's reluctance to act. It is, rather, enforcing Christ's victory over satan. It is the effective, fervent communication with the Creator of the Universe—in line with His will—which affects the balance of power in world affairs. Prayer transcends the dimensions of time and space and ushers us into the very throne room of God, worshiping, petitioning and interceding in that spiritual realm of the eternal now.

Prayer is sometimes *alleluia* (Psalm 150). It is sometimes telling God the details of our *needs* (Philippians 4:6). It is sometimes laboring in unutterable groans of *intercession* (Romans 8:26). It is the prayer of a sending church that releases power through His messengers in Asia, Africa, Europe, the Middle East and the Americas.

Prayer is the arena of spiritual warfare. Those who enter there are in touch with a world in need. Those who enter there regularly know the scars, but also the victory in battle.

I had progressed through the study on spiritual warfare with a group of Bible school students in India. I had a translator who had a good grasp on the English language as well as the material I was covering. The day came for me to teach on "the tactics of the enemy." I woke up early. I was so dizzy I could not get out of bed. They called me for breakfast, but I said I would skip it. I struggled to my feet, all the time rebuking the enemy. I was barely able to get dressed and "ready" for the day. I slowly walked to the auditorium. Once on the platform, to maintain my balance, I had to hold on to the sides of the chair. When I got up to speak, I told them I was so dizzy that I could hardly stand there. I said, "The enemy does not want us to learn about his tactics. You are looking at one of his efforts now! I need you to pray for me." They did. Oh, how they prayed! And I taught for seven hours that day, without a sign of dizziness. What satan had meant for evil, God turned into a valuable lesson on the effectiveness of prayer.

Prayer is where the action is—supporting and sustaining those on the fields of the world.

Yvonne's dad was ministering in Africa. He jumped down a small embankment and broke a rib, which punctured his lung. While he was in the hospital, one of his prayer warriors back home was awakened, "knowing" something was wrong. She prayed. Halfway around the world, he was healed instantly. Later, they compared notes to discover her prayer and his healing were at the exact same time.

It is vitally important for your cross-cultural worker to have a strong prayer support team every step of the way: from his calling to his church's approval, from his Biblical and cultural training to his developing his whole support team—all before he even arrives on the field. And that intercession must continue daily throughout his time on the field. And when he returns home!

> "Cross-cultural workers often have to deal with unfamiliar battle tactics."

All Christians are involved in spiritual warfare. Wherever they are aggressively battling the enemy, there is a greater vulnerability to his attacks. However, your cross-cultural worker often has to deal with battle tactics less familiar than those he faced back home. Where there is less Christian witness, there is greater oppression. Cultures more open to Eastern religions and animism are also more aware of the evil spirit world. Territory that satan has held for generations does not yield easily. Add to this your worker's adjustment to all the unknowns of his new culture, and you already have a sizable prayer list.

Because you may not have ever "been there," his prayer needs may seem so remote or unreal. Thus, you may sense a lack of being able to make your prayer specific.

Here is a prayer list to give you a good start in understanding the areas of need peculiar to a cross-cultural worker. When you communicate with him, ask which of these areas are vital to him. As you let him know of your commitment to sustain him in prayer, he will be happy to keep you informed of the more specific requests—especially if you ask in later communication with him how your prayers were answered.

- Adjusting to the new language, different foods, new customs, difficult climate.
- Protection in travel, health, accidents, dangerous situations.
- Parents' concern for their children's health, schooling, friendships.
- Housing accommodations, lack of privacy, differences in living standards, lack of accustomed conveniences.
- Loneliness, homesickness, lack of accustomed fellowship with others.
- Interpersonal relationships, dealing with one's own (and others') prejudice, selfishness.
- Dependence on the faithfulness of others to meet one's financial needs.
- Effectiveness in ministry, whatever the assignment.
- Functioning of the tools of ministry. (It is amazing how computers can crash at the wrong time! Yet, is there ever a right time for them to crash?)
- Lack of visible results; the "plowing, planting and watering" stages can go on for years!
- The people being ministered to, the national Christians, the leaders of the country.
- Need for stability, wisdom, compassion, self-discipline, boldness, power, love, to be filled with the Spirit of God.

A Model Prayer

Jo Shetler had completed the translation of the Balangao New Testament. A flourishing church had been established. She was now called back to the Philippines to be a speaker at the Balangao Bible Conference. Her subject was prayer.

She said that her prayer life had consisted of "... all we ask God to do, such as heal our sicknesses, provide money to put children through school, give the ability to learn a language, translate Scripture and interact well with people.

"Then I decided to pray the prayers of Paul, David, and others in the Bible. I copied them out and started in. Wow, did I ever get a surprise! Those people weren't asking God for the same things I was! These 'model prayers' from Scripture seemed to center more directly on God and His program, rather than on people and their plans."

"Use the prayers of the Bible as models for your prayers."

Read all the articles on prayer; read all the books about prayer. But when you are done, read, study and use as models the prayers of the Bible!

One of the prayers of Paul fits perfectly the needs of the cross-cultural worker. He was praying the prayer for the Christians in Colossae, but note how adaptable it is to the needs of any missionary.

Even before he prayed, Paul twice assured those at Colossae that he was constantly praying for them. Look at Colossians 1:3 and 9: "praying always for you ...; for this cause we also, since the day we heard of it, do not cease to pray for you."

Everyone who is interested in your missionary will at one time or another breathe a prayer for him. Certainly the financial support team will pray as they write out their checks: "Lord, may they use this money wisely," or "Lord, do they really need this money more than I do?"

The communication support team will no doubt pray that the missionary will have time to read the email that they wrote and that it will minister to him.

The moral support team will surely whisper a prayer as they

see your missionary's picture on the church bulletin board or when the pastor leads in a congregational prayer for him.

But if you are going to be a part of your missionary's prayer support team, your commitment must be more on the level of Paul's statement: "... we also since the day we heard of it, do not cease to pray for you."

Here, then, is a prayer that you can use as a model as you pray for your cross-cultural worker, filling in the details of his specific personality and ministry needs:

"That you might be filled with the knowledge of His will."
Colossians 1:9

Once a worker arrives on the field, he is bombarded with an overwhelming array of ministry opportunities. Even if a predetermined job description has been established, there is always one more assignment to fit into the schedule. When joining a team that is short-handed by illness, or workers on home assignment, or lack of laborers for an expanding ministry, your cross-cultural worker may be faced with appeals to take on "just a little bit more."

Out of that mass of good deeds, your worker must discern those that were "beforehand determined that he should walk in" (Ephesians 2:10).

Once he has heard God's will, a corollary prayer is for him to judiciously share with his supervisor that, in order to maintain his sanity, he must say "no" to certain opportunities.

"... in all wisdom and spiritual understanding."
Colossians 1:9

It is noteworthy that throughout Scripture these two qualities of the Christian life are always twins—one with the other. *Wisdom* can be defined as "the ability to see things from God's perspective" and *understanding* as "the ability to know how to make that Godly perspective work out in day-to-day living."

One missionary statesman wisely said, "The only ones who know everything about missions are those who have been on the field less than six months!" Bombarded with cultural distinctives, worlds apart from his own culture, and quite possibly faced with methods that have become bogged down in tradition, your worker continually needs to see things from God's perspective—things pertaining to family life, ministry, relationship with nationals, economy of time and energy, finances, personal devotions, relationships with ministers on his team and those of other groups.

It is not for nothing that Solomon urges: "Get wisdom, and with all your getting, get understanding" (Proverbs 4:7)!

As your prayers "bind the strong man" (Matthew 12:29) so your worker can have a clear vision from God's vantage point of eternal values—as your prayers elevate your missionary to realize he is "seated with Christ in heavenly places" (Ephesians 2:6), he must now understand how to make all of that happen in the daily affairs of his life.

Days—even weeks—of extended travel away from home wreak havoc with scheduled family time. Dare we use God's money to take a vacation? How do I tell the nationals that we aren't going to use US dollars to build their building—that it is better for the local congregation to trust God for the provision? How do I not violate my doctrinal distinctives, yet develop a working relationship with others in the Body of Christ? These and a thousand questions bombard your worker's life and demand an understanding heart (1 Kings 3:9). To see things from God's perspective is one thing (wisdom); to know how to make them work out in your missionary's every day life is another (understanding).

You can see how this prayer for wisdom and understanding could consume hours of intercession as you wage war against the enemy, and help your missionary live in the victory Christ won for him on Calvary.

"That you might walk worthy of the Lord unto all pleasing."   Colossians 1:10

Phillips' translation puts it, "That your outward lives which men see may bring credit to your Master's Name." Watchman Nee said, "If you want to be a missionary to China, plan on wearing a 'learner's permit' around your neck for the first ten years!" Due to diverse cultural distinctives and your cross-cultural worker's lack of ability to communicate deeply, it is often the love of Christ working through his lifestyle that gives the Gospel message.

Another perspective, of course, is that "What you are doing speaks so loudly, I can't hear what you are saying!" When your worker's actions differ from his words, it will be his actions that the people among whom he ministers will believe.

The enemies of the cross gave the name "Christian" (little Christ) to the believers in Antioch (Acts 11:26). It was a dirty word then, but since the followers of the Way were living epistles, known and read by all men (2 Corinthians 3:2), they were easily identifiable. Are we so easy to identify?

A team of college students walked into a remote village in Central America where there were no Christians. Their job was to paint a school building a previous team had built. They were excited to share the Lord, so the weight of their luggage and equipment seemed light.

As they entered the square, they were met by the village captain. He told them his people had heard all they needed to about 'this Man, Jesus' from the last team. "We don't want to hear another word you might have to say. Just paint our school building as you said you would. We will watch you. When you have finished, we will let you know if we want your Jesus."

The team knew their outward lives would be living epistles, "the Word written on fleshly tablets of the heart" (2 Corinthians 3:2-3). All they believed about the Word was put to the test in that village.

Those students "walked worthy of the Lord"; when they were ready to leave, ten people including the village captain trusted in Christ as their Savior!

"... being fruitful unto every good work." Colossians 1:10

There are two considerations for prayer here:

1) That your missionary will be involved in "good work." Unfortunately, there are thousands of man-hours of effort that aren't even aimed at decisive points of battle. Your prayers of intercession will open his eyes to where to spend his energy and that he knows he has the energy and ability to do it. Your prayers will release the Spirit's guidance in developing a specific strategy "unto every good work" for your missionary.

2) Thus, being involved in good works, you and your worker are interested in seeing "fruit that remains." To birth a child is (to say the least) hard work! Yet, the Word says, "for the joy that a man is born, the pain is forgotten" (John 16:21). To raise a child in godliness is incomparably more difficult.

To be used of the Spirit to birth a child spiritually and cross-culturally is hard work! To nurture that child to maturity demands the patient endurance of years.

It is true that one sows, another waters, but the Lord gives the increase (1 Corinthians 3:6). The only "good work" for a missionary is not just the salvation of the lost. Pulling a drunken "baby" Christian out of the ditch and have him vomit on your missionary can require your prayers to keep him joyfully serving the Lord.

"... and increasing in the knowledge of God."
Colossians 1:10

The personal devotional life of your worker is at stake here. On the field there are many factors that can lead to spiritual drought:

1) Your worker may become so busy "working for the Lord" that there is no time for personal intake. He does not take the time to be still and hear from the Lord. His head can

still nod at the appropriate times; his public prayers can still sound holy; his teaching can still be most proper! Unfortunately, though, *he knows* the life of the Spirit is gone.

2) Loneliness haunts many cross-cultural workers. More susceptible, of course, are single adults. This can lead to seeking inappropriate relationships, which can lead to spiritual dryness.

One single woman was continually being harassed by the married people about "getting married." Unfortunately, she found relief from this pressure in a local bar! A kind, married couple became her confidants.

3) Expectations of the people back home are not met. Some think, "We are paying the bill. We want to see some results!" And generally those "results" are in the number of conversions.

One friend wrote from a very difficult field. He knew that his major work would be "breaking up fallow ground" and had communicated that to his support team members. But, after six months the people back home were wanting "statistics"! He had none. He was discouraged.

4) Failure in task takes its toll on some. Discouragement debilitates. This downward spiral of morale is slippery. At the bottom of the slide are many spiritually depleted field workers. Often these burned-out workers do not realize they should go home. They become an embarrassment to the mission endeavor, a drain on the energies of others who are trying to help them and a dismal blot on the testimony of God's Church in the world!

5) Disillusionment can bring awful frustration, which in turn may lead to spiritual drought. In the mission process there are many tasks that aren't very glamorous—cleaning the grease trap outside the kitchen door, keeping inventory on radio parts, or being reviled by a drunken street-sleeper.

6) One may become discontented with other workers. "Discontent" is putting it mildly! "Radical interpersonal relationship problems" might be more accurate. This is the number one cause of missionary failure. Why? Because Jesus said, "They [the ones your worker has gone out to seek and to save] will know we are His disciples by our love *for one another*" (John 13:35). So here is a major area of attack by the enemy: If he can destroy our unity he will destroy our testimony!

> **"Your prayers build a hedge of protection around your friend."**

Your prayers and the united intercession of the prayer support team for your cross-cultural worker will put a hedge of protection around him (Ezekiel 22:30), will guard his thoughts (Philippians 4:4-7) and will give him the wisdom of a peacemaker in those tough interpersonal situations (James 3:13-18).

"... strengthened with all might, according to His glorious power." Colossians 1:11

In Acts 1:4 and 8 Jesus gave clear instruction to His disciples to wait for the power of the Holy Spirit to come upon them. It's a jungle out there! It is insane to step into cross-cultural outreach ministry without "His glorious power." It is imperative to have a vital, personal, alive, active, growing, dynamic, real relationship with the third Person of the Godhead, the Holy Spirit.

My wife leads teams on prayer walks in spiritually dark places. The atmosphere is oppressive. The powers of darkness are permeating the very air they breathe. They find it of value to pray as Paul did: "I will pray in the spirit and with understanding" (I Corinthians 14:15).

Intercede for your cross-cultural worker that he would be continually being "filled with the Spirit" (Ephesians 5:18). Pray that he will daily "mind the things of the Spirit" (Romans 8). Life and ministry in a second culture (actually, we all walk in an alien world!) hold challenges foreign to your worker but not to the Spirit of God. As you pray, the Spirit of truth will guide him into all truth (John 16:13).

"... unto all patience and longsuffering with joyfulness."
Colossians 1:11

Yvonne and I, and three of our children, were ready to leave Brazil. Because we had stayed several months over the two-year visa issued, the federal government in Brasilia had provided us with a letter assuring us that all was in order for us to leave. However, at the time of departure, we had to present that letter and our passports (which did show an expired visa) to the state official. He looked at me and said, "You are in our country illegally! That will be a $500 fine!" We spent three days returning to that official trying to convince him (speaking through an translator, of course) to let us go. Finally, finding a way to let him "save face", he came up with an idea and he stamped our exit visa.

Missionaries are more than familiar with bank lines, gas lines, food lines and delays in mail deliveries, material deliveries and baby deliveries! Patience and longsuffering are critical!

But there is another phrase: "with joyfulness." Yes, your worker might in stoicism realize he has no alternative than to wait. The issue is, can he brush off the

"Patience, *with* joyfulness!"

cobwebs of delay with joyfulness? Can the joy of the Lord be his strength as after a two-hour wait in line he steps up to the bank teller's window and is told, "Sorry, we are going on strike right now!"

One day another friend went to his bank. He saw that they were going to do some construction. He thought—this is great. They are going to put in another teller window. However, on his next visit, they had enlarged the waiting area!

Yes, your prayers as vials of sweet incense intercede for him

before the Father day and night, meting out to him the measure
of grace sufficient for any trial. Prayer is where the action is!

"... Giving thanks unto the Father." Colossians 1:12

Paul enjoined the Christians in Philippi to "Be anxious
for nothing; but in everything by prayer and supplication
with thanksgiving let your requests be made known to God"
(Philippians 4:6). A thankful attitude reveals a heart that is right
with God. Every time you enter your arena of prayer for your
friend, enter "His gates with thanksgiving in your heart and
enter His courts with praise" (Psalm 100:4).

The pressures of the mission field can produce in your
worker something other than a thankful attitude. The difficult
living conditions can say, "It's not fair!" The depleting of
finances each month can shout, "I deserve better!" The lack of
apparent spiritual response can cry, "These people are not worth
my time!" The breakdown in health can mull over, "I guess God
didn't really call me to this work!"

Your prayers can be used to challenge your missionary with
Mordecai's words: "Who knows but that for such an hour as
this you have been called to the Kingdom" (Esther 4:14)? Your
prayers can be used to help your cross-cultural worker identify
with Paul: "For I reckon that the sufferings of this present time
are not worthy to be compared with the glory which shall be
revealed in us" (Romans 8:18). Your prayers can be used to stir
the resources that will build in your field worker an attitude of
thankfulness: "It is a privilege to be about our Father's business."

In-the-Gap Praying

> *"And I sought for a man among them that should
> make up the hedge, and stand in the gap before me
> for the land, that I should not destroy it: but I found
> none."* Ezekiel 22:30

The "gap" mentioned in Ezekiel has been used to express
a number of concepts. Prophetically Jesus came to bridge the

chasm between God and man. As an appeal to people to go to the mission fields of the world, filling in the "gap" of front-line workers is critical. There are cultural gaps between the missionary and the people group he is trying to reach.

In the context of Ezekiel, though, "in the gap" speaks more directly of the role of an intercessor—one who forms a barrier (a hedge) between God (who is speaking) and "the land, that I should not destroy it."

"I looked for a man...." Abraham

"Stand in the gap for your friend."

became that man: "God, will you not spare the city for fifty righteous men? Forty-five? Forty? Thirty? Twenty? Ten? Far be it from You to slay the righteous with the wicked.... Shall not the Judge of all the earth do right" (Genesis 18)? Those are powerful words for one who had "taken upon himself to speak to the Lord, seeing [he was] but dust and ashes!" He stood in the gap.

"I looked for a man...." Moses became that man: "And Moses besought the face of the Lord his God, and said, 'Lord, why does Your wrath wax hot against *Your* people?'" Just four verses earlier, in His anger God had called them Moses' people! After two more verses of intercession, "the Lord repented of the evil which He thought to do unto His people" (Exodus 32:11-14).

Another time Moses even more boldly said: "Yet now, if you will forgive their sin...; and if not, blot me, I pray Thee, out of Your book which You have written" (Exodus 32:32)! Read Deuteronomy, Chapter Nine for a review of the many times Moses stood in the gap for His people. Moses was definitely an "in-the-gap" intercessor!

"I looked for a man...." Aaron became that man (Numbers 16). Nehemiah became that man (Nehemiah). Jesus became that Man (John 17). Paul became that man (Romans 9). Others through the generations of time have become that man, that woman who stood in the gap.

And today Scripture still declares the voice of God—which perhaps is saying to you, "I am looking for you to make up the hedge, to stand in the gap!"

A battle is raging for the souls of mankind. In the book of Job, we have been given some insight into the spiritual realm from which this war emanates.

Job had arrived! He was rich. He was famous. He was perfect and upright. He feared God and hated evil. At least, this is what the human eye could see.

Behind the scenes of this visible world, however, is the real world. And satan saw the hedge complete—not only around Job, but "about his house, and about all that he has on every side" (Job 1:1-10). Two excellent novels, *This Present Darkness* and *Piercing the Darkness* by Frank Peretti, give thought-provoking possibilities to the subtleties of this behind-the-scenes war.

The "accuser of the brethren" (Revelation 12:10) is "going to and fro in the earth, and is walking up and down in it seeking whom he may devour" (1 Peter 5:8). When he sees the breach in the hedge, the broken-down walls, the secret thoughts of sin, he is able to enter the minds and hearts of men with ease.

Even when that hedge is complete around a man, satan presents himself before God. It's those "perfect ones" he wants to get. So God, knowing his thoughts, says, "satan, have you set your heart on my servant, Job" (Job 1:8)?

This is one of the works of the enemy: To set his heart on even the elect, if it were possible (Matthew 24:24). Jesus said, "Peter, satan desires to have you to sift you like wheat; but I have prayed for you" (Luke 22:31). Satan and a third of the host of heaven who rebelled against God with him are out to destroy, to whatever degree and with whatever diabolical consequences they can contrive.

Picture the scene in that heavenly throne room, that secret place you enter boldly to obtain mercy and grace to help in your time of need (Hebrews 4:16). Not only are you in God's presence as you intercede for the "mercy and grace" your cross-cultural worker needs, but also present is the adversary. Whether the enemy of our souls is telling the truth about our weaknesses or lying about us, he is using any tactic in his fiendish arsenal to break through the hedge and rush through the gap. This is not only for your friend, but for you and the prayer support team, as well. If he can destroy the prayer warriors, he has destroyed the front line of defense.

Unbelief is the single most serious factor that breaks down the hedge. God is looking for a team, for a woman, for a man "to make up the hedge, to stand in the gap before Me for the land (on behalf of the people), that I should not destroy it: but I found none!" And, in the Ezekiel account, it can be assumed that destruction came!

May it not be said of us on that awesome judgment day that He was calling from among us—a prayer support team to stand in the gap—but He found none! Rather may He say, "Well done, thou good and faithful servant. Enter thou into the joy of the Lord" (Matthew 25:21)!

One of the strongest weapons to bind the work of the enemy is the intercessory, effectual, fervent prayer of a committed, united team of believers (James 5:16).

The prayer support team should never be limited in number, nor can we be certain whose prayer and when that prayer will be effective.

One morning while trying to watch my son's surgery, I "decided" to faint! In the process, I sustained a fractured skull and serious brain concussion. For three weeks I lay flat in bed and lived from one pain pill to the next. I was praying! My wife was praying! Our children were praying! Plus, all the missionaries in the area were praying! Without my knowledge, one morning my wife got on the ham radio to solicit additional prayer from the team back home. She contacted our pastor's wife just as she was preparing to go to a church prayer meeting. Following that prayer of intercession, I never took another pain pill. I had no more pain. Why our prayers, over that period of three weeks, "didn't work", I'll never know. But I certainly rejoice that somebody's prayer (maybe it was the prayers of all of us, combined!) was submitted to the will of the Father, and healing came.

FASTING AND PRAYER

In a trilogy of instruction in what has become known as the Sermon on the Mount, Jesus said, "When you give..., when you pray..., when you fast." He presumes that we will fast. He follows each injunction with contrasting instruction: "Don't do it this way; but do do it this way" (Matthew 6:1-18).

Unfortunately, today what most Christians know about fasting and food is *fast food!* The Biblical significance of fasting, however, is so profound throughout the Old and New Testaments that for us to be ignorant of or indifferent toward its place in a Christian's life is equal to "spiritual starvation!"

When you give ...
When you pray ...
When you fast ...

"But I'll starve to death!" is exactly the way many Christians respond. Therefore, we need to know the "what, why, when, and how" of fasting.

What is fasting? Both in the secular sense and in the Biblical sense, fasting means abstaining from food. It is more than just to stop eating, however. A total fast is abstaining from all food and drink (Exodus 34:28). A normal fast allows the intake of drink (Luke 4:2). A limited fast indicates restriction of certain types of foods (Daniel 10:2-3). Prayer and care must be taken in choosing the type of fast that God wants us to enter.

Why should we fast? Because Jesus told us to. Isaiah gave clear spiritual and physical purposes for the exercise of fasting:

a) Spiritual: "To loose the bands of wickedness, to undo the heavy burdens, to let the oppressed go free, and that you break every yoke."

b) Physical: "To deal your bread to the hungry, to bring the poor that are afflicted to your home, to clothe the naked, and to be available to help your own relatives" (Isaiah 58:6-7).

When should we fast? Definitely not when Christ the Bridegroom is around. "But when He is taken up from among them, then they will fast" (Matthew 9:14-15). As we still await the return of the Bridegroom, now is the time for fasting!

How should we fast? Definitely "not as the hypocrite who puts on a gloomy face and neglects his appearance in order to be seen fasting by men. Rather, brush your hair and wash your face so that nobody knows that you are fasting. Let it be a secret between you and your Father. For He knows all secrets and will reward you" (Matthew 6:17-18).

Because our bodies are meant to take in food, and there is no spiritual merit in injuring our bodies through fasting, there are other important "do's and don'ts" we must consider as we enter and conclude our fast. One of the finest works on the subject of fasting is Arthur Wallis' classic, *God's Chosen Fast.*

When prayer and fasting are practiced in concert, they present a unique and powerful duo. Incorporate the practice of fasting with your prayer for your missionary.

What a privilege that God allows us to participate in His Plan of the Ages by coming boldly before Him, interceding on behalf of the lost of the world as well as for the workers who have gone out to the fields of the world. If God be for us, who can be against us (Romans 8:31)? What an unequal contest it seems!

It is prayer that links the missionary enterprise to the irresistible power of God. Prayer is the decisive point on which the battle turns. The mightiest weapon we can use is the weapon of prayer—potent, powerful, prevailing prayer, the prayer of faith against which the adversary has no effective counter weapon.

Yvonne and I are aware of the intensity of true prayer warfare. With this in mind, each year we personally release our prayer team from their commitment. Of course, we also encourage them to "re-up" for another year of intercession. Having them make an annual commitment keeps the seriousness of prayer clear in their minds.

Unfortunately, through the years we have lost some valuable prayer warriors. We cannot over-emphasize the importance of praying with someone and praying for your own protection in this most vital area of care.

One of our faithful prayer warriors called my wife. She said that she could no longer pray for us when we traveled. She explained that on each trip when she would commit to pray, her daughter would get sick with asthma, even requiring hospitalization! Yvonne asked her if she first prayed for protection for herself and her family before interceding for us. She admitted that she hadn't and agreed to pray for the next trip. She prayed for her family's protection before entering into intercession for us. Her daughter has not experienced the same problem again.

"Pray without ceasing" (1 Thessalonians 5:17).

IT HAPPENED THIS WAY IN SACRAMENTO

Prayer support for our missionaries is much harder to talk about than the other areas of care. For example, in regards to financial support, we have the concrete evidence every month when the checks come into the church office that the people are following through with their commitment.

Prayer support is a little more difficult. There is not that tangible "something" to assure us that they are following through with their commitment. Nor is it easy in our busy lifestyle to commit the time to pray for missionaries. It takes only minutes to write a check. Or, today, only a one-time "commitment" to tell the bank to send a check every month! Prayer, however, takes time! So, in this area, we need to work harder.

One element of prayer support is an awareness of needs. You need a good system for making needs known. You can do this in several ways:

1) Everyone committed to support our missionaries in prayer is encouraged to have one clock in their house set to the time of their ministry location. When we wake up at 7 a.m. and realize what time it is for them, it can prompt us

to pray with an increased awareness of what they are doing at that time. It might even be a different day there!

2) Our missionaries have a monthly newsletter they send to supporters with a specific section summarizing their prayer needs. This portion of the letter can be printed out, highlighted and stuck to the refrigerator with a photo magnet that they received when they made the commitment to pray.

3) Two prayer chains have been formed. A prayer chain is simply a list of names and phone numbers. As a prayer request is made known via phone call or email, the person at the top of the list is notified. He phones the next person on the list who then relays the message to the next person and so on until all are made aware of the need.

Two prayer chains were developed for this reason: It was felt that there may be times when a need would arise that was of such a personal nature that it might be best if only the Core Group and a few others determined by our missionaries would know about it in detail. The second prayer chain would receive that prayer request in more general terms. Other requests may be given to both groups.

Another element of prayer support is to be able to intercede as led by the Holy Spirit without even knowing the needs. Or, perhaps, the information we receive indicating their needs aren't really the needs at all! It is necessary for us then, by the Spirit, to perceive the real needs as we get together in intercession for them and the people among whom they're ministering. We're always trying to expand our prayer so we include the people group. Our missionaries will be coming home one day, and it seems only reasonable we would develop hearts for the needs of those people now so we can keep praying for God's activity among them for years to come.

One way we are attempting to increase the effectiveness of our prayers was expressed in a recent email we sent out to all our prayer supporters. In it we asked for volunteers to make a weekly commitment to fast and pray for one hour. We suggested a dinner fast (actually starting right after lunch) with a prayer time following in the evening. We also stated that if they felt led to commit to a longer fast or even a partial fast—that was certainly between them and the Lord.

Prayer is truly a powerful weapon to be used in the spiritual conflicts encountered in cross-cultural ministry. Yet again, there are other aspects of your worker's life that must be considered. He, as a cultural being, will want you to keep in touch with him through communication support.

(In addition to the individual study below, see the **Group Leader's Guide** for Chapter Five beginning on page 205.)

FOR YOUR PERSONAL INVOLVEMENT

- Keep a record for one week of the prayers you pray. Is there a good mixture of praise, personal petition, intercession and thanksgiving?

- Study the prayers of several Bible characters. (Be sure to include the publican's prayer in Luke 18:13!) Or read through all the prayers of one person. Identify if each is a prayer of thanksgiving, praise, personal petition or intercession. Become familiar with the way the prayer sounds. Compare (or contrast) them with your style of praying.

- Locate, read and study the nineteen recorded prayers of Jesus.

- Begin or become part of a missions prayer group where you can learn to participate in the power of united prayer.

- Read Arthur Wallis' book, *God's Chosen Fast*.

ACTION STEPS

By the time you have read Chapter Five, completed the *For Your Personal Involvement* section and participated in a discussion group, you should ...

- More and more, use the prayers of the Bible as models for your prayers. Avoid as much as possible the ever-popular "gimmie" prayers.

- Be able to decide if prayer support is a commitment you can make to your missionary. If you can, contact him, letting him know of that commitment and of your desire to be kept informed of his prayer needs.

- Practice the Christian discipline of fasting.

- Pray without ceasing!

- Multiply yourself. Actively look for others in your circle of relationships who have or who might develop a heart for prayer.

CHAPTER 6

Communication Support

"Lord willing, I plan to send Timothy to you soon so that I may be comforted when I know how you are doing."
Philippians 2:19

“ I HAD ZILCH KNOWLEDGE of missions and no preparation whatsoever! I knew God wanted me to go to Paris, but even that was only confirmed in my heart after I arrived there. My home church's 'policy' was to lay hands on you, say a prayer and wave, 'Good-bye!' My home fellowship group said they would write to me and pray for me. I faithfully sent an email update about every five weeks. I received one response from them the first year and one the second!

"Lack of communication further hit me as soon as I arrived. I was to work with another missionary from my church who was helping to equip lay leaders in a new church near the Latin Quarter. When I got there, I found out that he had moved to another city!

"A local national church took me in. I began learning servanthood in a cross-cultural setting. Sweeping, cleaning toilets, dusting, sorting clothes and running errands were my first assignments. Though I had majored in French in college, I had to regain my ability in the language. Then I began teaching in their day school for children.

"Lack of communication also hit my finances! I arrived

in Paris with $15 and a promise of a temporary place to stay (remember, I had had no training). I was never taught how to raise financial support. I had not communicated my needs before I left, nor in my emails once I was gone. I thought it was 'bad' to talk about money. Now I know I should give full information and allow others to share in His ministry that way.

"I got a small check from a friend through my church the first month. Well into the second month I called my brother to call my church to see if any money had come in for me and if they had mailed it. Only $45 had come in and it had been mailed, returned for postage, and mailed again! Anyway, I moved ten times that first year because I had to live wherever I could without paying rent.

"By then I had come to accept it: This is missionary life. Then I met Bill and Louise. It began when they offered to help me financially. I felt bad because their church was supporting them and they were using some of it to help me. Yet, my church was doing nothing.

"As I got to know them better, I saw that not only were their finances in order, but a whole communication network was in place. Regular emails. Frequent 'care' packages. Phone calls of friendship (not of desperation, like mine).

"But I really saw how it could be when their church's cross-cultural coordinator, John, came to visit them. It was just a one-day visit as he was in Europe on other business, but I saw real caring. He had prepared a special Bible study that he said the Lord had given him just for them. He brought a computer banner saying, 'We really do miss you!' It had personal notes scribbled all over it. There were special goodies for their children.

"I came to realize that to the extent the communication, prayer and financial support was strong from their sending church—to that extent their ministry was strong. John said I could call on them any time there was a need. He didn't know the extent of my hurting (or did he?). I received a form *Newsletter* once a year from my church telling me what they were doing (yes, I was even listed as one of their 'accomplishments'!), but they never once asked me how I was doing! I had a lot of anger and hurt inside towards my church before coming back because I felt they didn't care.

"After two years I did come home. And I realized the misunderstanding was as much a lack of my communication as theirs. I was open with my home fellowship. I learned that they thought the church was supporting me financially and I thought they knew of my condition and need! We just hadn't communicated!

"I got some good training in communication skills. I learned to be open in sharing my needs for communication as well as for prayer, finances and the other areas of support.

"I am back in Paris now. No, I don't expect a visit from anyone from my church with banners and goodies. However, I now have an established foundation of a strong and growing support team from my home fellowship and other individuals in my church and family. And we're communicating! May God be praised!"

It is hard to imagine the importance of communication from home until you have "been there." When a person or family arrives on the field to establish their new routine, real loneliness can set in—a feeling of isolation, of being out of touch with—everybody! A new missionary can feel, "They have forgotten me!" "They aren't communicating" might be interpreted: "They don't care! I'm out of their sight—and therefore out of their mind! And I am going out of mine!"

One family recently returned to Israel, this time with two children. The wife recalls, "The first two weeks I was filled with guilt for doing this to my children. I had taken them away from the grandparents who cherish them and whom they adore. I had taken them away from Sesame Street, a wonderful library, swimming lessons and food they love. I had taken them away from carpeted floors to fall on, trashless parks with grass instead of broken glass, cool weather, Sunday school—away from friends, drinkable water that doesn't make them sick, a familiar doctor I can trust, a car instead of a bus or having to walk in the blazing sun and a mommy with lots of energy, patience and joy!

"Well," she says, "a phone call from Amy back in my home town revealed that she had felt the same way when she first went to Greece. I still wasn't completely convinced that I was doing the best for my boys; but if Amy got through it—and her kids are great ... and I do trust God Who is my Father and theirs, Who only wants the best for us....

"After the call, I began to think, 'To tell the truth, David and Daniel seem to be adapting more quickly than I am! Two-year-old David even reminded me of a Hebrew word that I couldn't think of the other day. And Daniel has learned how to fall on these hard floors without getting a big bump on his head.'"

The missionary concludes, "Even my mother is handling this well. She recently encouraged me in a phone call: 'God wants you there, Mary. Your kids could get sick here, too. C'mon, toughen up!' It seems every time we get discouraged, some bit of communication comes through to encourage us!"

COMMUNICATING THROUGH WRITING

Paul did not have access to the telephone or fax, modern postal system, email or computer chat room, yet as a prolific New Testament writer, he knew the importance of personal communication. By whatever means you communicate with your missionary friend, a lot can be learned from Paul and other New Testament writers.

Paul's Letters are shot through with bits of personal comments.

- Requests for his support team to "bring his cloak when they come to him and the books (and if not enough room for everything) especially the parchments" (2 Timothy 4:13).

- An earnest appeal to "prepare your guest room for me" (Philemon 22).

- In his powerful letter to the Christians in Rome—that great treatise on grace—he devotes almost all of chapter 16 to personal messages. No less than 41 people are specifically mentioned. Tertius, who has been writing the Roman letter for Paul, might have gotten so excited about all this exchange of greetings that he leaned over and nudged Paul: "Paul, may I say 'Hi,' too?" For verse 22 reads, "I, Tertius, send my Christian greetings also!"

James personalized his short letter 17 times by referring to the dispersed tribes as "my brothers." John, when writing to his friend Gaius and again to "the elect lady", found it difficult to put into words all he wanted to say (2 John 12; 3 John 13). Yet in writing his Gospel he wanted a scroll the size of the whole world to write everything on his heart (John 21:25). Luke, for the sake of his friend Theophilus, "searched out diligently...from the highest to the smallest detail," to set in order the record of the Gospel of Christ and the Acts of the Apostles (Luke 1:1-4).

Peter and Paul found it not burdensome to remind their readers again and again of especially important things (2 Peter 1:12; Philippians 3:1). Jude, as he sat to write his brief Letter, intended to make it a light, happy rejoicing in their common salvation. But as he took pen in hand, the Spirit of God compelled him to exhort them to "earnestly contend for the faith" (Jude 3).

Whether on parchment or paper or through cyberspace, letter writing (even though we don't call it that anymore!) is the easiest, most common way of keeping in touch; it is the mainstay of communication.

WHAT TO COMMUNICATE

The content of your communication is vital. Say things that really matter. Not just "How are you? I am fine. Went to the store today. Had meat loaf for dinner." (Of course, they'll read anything from home! One time I caught myself reading *The Ladies Home Journal* just to be able to read something in English! But....)

Rather, share your thoughts and feelings—what is really going on in your life. How is God working in you? Be realistic and honest but don't use them as your counselor. Remember, you are *their* support.

Get involved in their lives on the field as much as you can. Express interest in the concerns of their hearts. Ask questions about their lives there and respond to what they have said in their previous communication to you. This is especially encouraging because it shows that you really read their updates and are interested enough for some follow-up conversation about it.

Yvonne and I have pledged to respond to every missionary email or paper newsletter we receive—and we receive 100-120 every month! As I read their message, I have already hit "reply".

> "In all of your communicating, you are *their* support."

My response is not as lengthy as theirs, but it lets them know I read it. Recently, I replied to one friend that I had even read the fine print of his email. Why he put this item in fine print, I don't know. He was letting us know that he was going to attend his 55th high school reunion. I was able to share our recent experience at my 55th reunion. If it is a paper newsletter, I have a pen in hand to jot down notes or circle specific thoughts I want to respond to. If they have an email address, they get an email!

Share how God is leading you to pray for them. Ask for their specific and personal prayer requests and updates on things about which you previously prayed.

Share a particularly meaningful sermon you just heard, church news or news about a mutual friend—only edifying news, of course!

In supporting missionaries serving in restricted-access countries where their ministry may be considered illegal, be sure to check with your church or mission agency for guidelines about communicating anything regarding Christian matters and ministry. Some suggest using "code words." It is my opinion that anyone interested in checking already knows the code words! Encrypted emails may be the answer; some servers say they are safe. Experience is showing us, though, that any method of protection has a way of becoming unprotected by those who want to break in! (Wikileaks!)

Don't forget to have your kids communicate with the children in your missionary family. This is good training for them to become aware of and involved in missions! Also, grandmas and grandpas, aunts and uncles: Keep in contact with your grandkids, nieces and nephews. They need to hear from you.

Let's look back at the Biblical writers referred to for some patterns for you to follow in your writing to or chatting with your cross-cultural workers:

Paul to the Romans: Use names to make the stories real. Instead of, "The whole church says 'Hi'!" give the names of specific people they know who said "Hi."

James to the dispersed tribes: Make it a friendly email, personalized with terms of endearment. Even though (or maybe, because) James had some tough things to say, he reminded them of the personal relationship uniting them. "Though miles separate us, we are still friends; you are not forgotten" is the feeling communicated when you make the communication personal.

John to Gaius and the "elect lady": The time will come when it is tough to sit down and write that email. You don't know what to say or how to say it. Probably the single greatest hindrance to writing is waiting for a big block of time. Don't wait—it will probably never come! Just sit down and do it! If you have a great idea to share and you are not at your computer, jot (or speak) a note to yourself as a reminder on your iPhone. Your missionary would probably appreciate short, frequent messages, anyway. Check with them; they'll tell you.

A missionary recalls, "One of my favorite letters came on John F. Kennedy Airport toilet paper, written while a support team friend was waiting for an international flight! The novelty of it assured me of the instant inspiration of the words written!"

John to readers of his Gospel: Don't feel that you have to write every word of every conversation of every friend of theirs for every day they are gone! Allow the Spirit to guide you to share those incidents and stories that would be uplifting, informative, motivating or challenging.

How you say things also has its impact. Consider the following contrast:

"Well, Jerry has taken your place and is doing such a great job with your home fellowship group. Everything is just fine without you." vs. "Wow! God's timing is so perfect. Just as He called you to Alma Ata, He has raised up Jerry to continue the good work you were doing with the home fellowship group."

Luke to Theophilus: Be accurate in your reporting to your friends. Distance and time and cultures already have their way of distorting facts. Memory blurs. You want to communicate a true report of what's going on among the people back home.

Peter and Paul to readers of their Epistles: Sometimes with Peter and Paul you will say, "I do not tire of reminding you again and again to be diligent in your personal devotion to God." Don't be afraid to encourage and exhort with the same themes and reminders often—as the Spirit directs you.

And I remind you again, potential communication support person: You are *their* support. Do not use them as your counselor or prayer support. We really do need each other, but find your support in other than your missionaries.

Jude to those called of God: As you get in the habit of regular communication, you will begin anticipating what you want to say. As you listen to the words of a new song, you will realize how that would minister to your friend. You jot them down. As you return to a familiar recreation site or a favorite restaurant, a pleasant memory inspires you to relate an incident. So you sit down to write the regular email you committed to do, just wanting to rejoice about the good things of life. But then don't be surprised if there is also a stirring in your soul as the Holy Spirit says, "I have an important message for you to share. Warn him to be on his guard against 'ungodly men who are bent on thwarting the grace of God'" (Jude 4).

OTHER WAYS OF COMMUNICATING

This need for contact with "home" is nothing new. You remember the story of David, away from his home in Bethlehem. In the heat of battle, he longed for a drink of water from his favorite well over by the city gate (2 Samuel 23:15). His son Solomon said, "As cold water to a thirsty soul, so is good news from a far land" (Proverbs 25:25). The need for news from back home isn't new at all, but our world has certainly advanced in its methods of communication.

The telephone, for example, lets you call anywhere in the world for from 1.5-25 cents a minute! You might not use this method as regularly as email, but even just once can be a really special treat. You can be led by the Spirit to call at a needy time in your missionary's life.

> "Regular communication says, 'You are not forgotten.'"

A communicating sender says, "One time I was reading a letter from our cross-cultural worker. It wasn't so much what the letter said (since it had been written two weeks before) as it was that the Spirit quickened my mind to understand her present need. I checked the time. It should be about 7 a.m. in Israel. She should still be at home. I dialed. On the second ring, I heard her voice. And we talked for a few minutes. What did we say? I don't remember! But she still talks about that phone call that came at just the right time!"

Providing your missionary with a satellite phone may be a solution for good communication in very remote areas.

Ham radio is an adventurous communication channel. If your worker is in a more remote part of the world, he may still be depending on this means of contact. He may have his own set or know a ham radio operator. If so, have him give you the call letters and the times he is usually on the air. Then find an operator in your area. These people are usually happy to set up a "phone patch" for you to talk with your friend—often free— around the world!

E-mail, Facebook, Twitter, Linkedin, Skype, interactive internet sites, chat rooms, blogs, cell phone texting … the list goes on … have become the communication medias of choice. But how carefully we must choose in using these popular means of exchange. Oh, the volumes of words that can so easily flow off the tips of our fingers. And once it is out there in cyberspace, it's out there! Or, a careless word that is being listened to by their host government. In one restricted country, a phone call was even interrupted, "Please speak in English so I can understand you." The government worker who had tapped the phone knew English, but not the language in which the missionary and his support person were communicating.

Then, there are those "forwarded attachments!" The plethora of stories—many recycled four or five times—that fill cyberspace with their "inspiration." Many of them are really good, but before you press those two or three keys necessary to rush that message off to your friend, consider these three questions: 1) Is it something that will really minister to a current need in his life? (That answer might come in prayer.) 2) Does he have the time to read yours, and theirs, and all the others? (The answer is probably, No!) 3) How much will it cost him to download all those "neat" graphics, videos or audios? What will the cost be, if he loses his connection and has to start downloading over again? (Not worth it, he may say as he deletes your email.)

Communicate through photos. Attach a photo now and then with your email. But, again, be very careful and sensitive in sending high-resolution photos. It may be easy for you, but so expensive for him to receive and download, if he is able to at all.

A missionary recalls, "When we were on the field, we had a wall of pictures of friends and family. It was great to see their smiling faces. It was a lingering point for memories and prayer."

One of the missionary's sending team adds, "We have our own wall of cork arranged as the continents of the world. Over a hundred pictures (updated as they send new ones) place our missionary friends in their respective countries. It is for us, too, a location for prayer and memories of when they were in our house."

Video camcorders can be inexpensive and offer endless communication possibilities. Let your field worker rejoin the home fellowship meeting by recording it and other church get-togethers. Update your worker with a traveling tour of what's going on in your town. Record a family gathering. Interview new people as they come out of church, and introduce him to these newcomers. Or, with people your missionary knows, just come up to them and say, "Hey, in 20 words or less, what do you want to say to ——?" (Name your missionary.) Have the "roving mike" catch their first words—even their sputtering cry, "I don't know what to say!" Have a video camera at your next potluck dinner. Conduct a survey of any

> **"Fill their ears with the sounds they miss the most."**

ridiculous thing, such as: "In your opinion, if a Hottentot tot is taught to talk 'ere the tot can totter, ought the Hottentot tot be taught to say aught or not, or what ought to be taught her?" If that isn't enough for a few laughs for your missionary family, you might want to give them the second verse: "If, to hoot and to toot be taught to a Hottentot tot by a Hottentot tutor, ought the Hottentot tutor get hot if the Hottentot tot hoots and toots at the Hottentot tutor?" Okay, that might be a bit much!

Fill their ears with the sounds of the kids' choir or crickets chirping or frogs croaking, or the din of the freeway at rush hour—if that's what they miss.

Better than sending your creative work as an attachment, burn a DVD, and put it in the mail.

There are excellent Christian DVDs for kids. What you send may be the only viewing your workers' children can watch since in many countries television is often as or more explicit than in North America. There are, of course, good entertaining DVDs for adults, as well. Send CDs of special programs, ceremonies and sermons.

One organization has dedicated itself to providing CDs,

Videos, DVDs and audio books for missionaries at reduced prices. You may be able to purchase them through other Internet outlets, but with Mount Carmel, you can be assured of excellent Christian content. (www.mountcarmel.com)

For powerful Bible study on "every" text and theme, order from the Audio Catalog of free CDs from Firefighters for Christ: www.firefighters.org. Have them download the growing list of studies from ERI's ACTS Media Library: www.eri.org.

Some churches schedule a quarterly Sunday morning Skype session with their missionaries. Some focus the before service PowerPoint on their missionaries. Some take the time during the service to highlight a family on the mission field. The diverse means of communication today offer unlimited opportunity to relate with your missionaries.

I visited one church that has a computer with a touch screen in the foyer. They have a map of the world as the home page with the names and pictures of their missionaries in their various countries. When they touch a picture, an email comes up. They can send a message instantly. If the family is in a restricted country, of course, proper precautions are taken, such as the email will go to the missions pastor for "sanitizing" before he sends it on to the missionary.

Provide a web site for your missionary friend. There are organizations which will, for a small or no fee, allow your missionary friend to set up a web page. He can provide you (and his whole support team) with any creative communication he has the time to develop. You can become his "web servant."

A "care" package is a great idea. Of course, check first with the post office and with your missionary or agency on what may be sent. Find out how to label packages properly. It is amazing what you can put even in a letter envelope, thus making the shipping easier. Determine what your shipping costs plus their duty costs will be, otherwise you might send a package that costs double or triple what it is worth.

There are many items that will communicate your love: new books, music and Bible study CDs. One cross-cultural worker once mentioned that he really enjoys the Sunday sports section of his local newspaper. A loyal friend now mails it to him every week! (All newspapers are not yet on the Internet!) Sometimes even the little things that seem like nothing to us—a package of salad dressing mix or chili powder—are a delightful surprise if your missionaries live where those items are not available.

But don't be surprised if their tastes have changed. Ask them what their needs and their wants are now that they have been on the field. No matter how mundane the request, if it will minister to them, send it!

With each team that Yvonne leads, she asks the missionaries she will visit for a "wish list". Each team member lets their church and circle of friends know of these needs (sometimes wants). All check-in luggage is reserved to carry these items to the field.

Personal visits, of course, are the ultimate in communication. Paul longed to see his support team. Then he thanked them profusely when they sent a representative to minister to his needs. (Read Philippians 2:25-30; 4:15-18, for examples.)

One church takes a tour to Israel each year. Their missionaries in Greece and Turkey have the opportunity every other year to spend this time with their friends from back home—in Israel! The church pays the missionaries' fares to come from their place of ministry to Israel for those ten days of fellowship and vacation.

The missions pastor of one church regularly travels to the locations of the church's missionaries to put "new heart" in them and to encourage them in the Lord.

Even if you or one from your fellowship cannot make the visit, if you know of someone going to your worker's location or nearby, you can encourage that traveler to visit your missionary, to hand-carry a message or package of love and concern. On the other hand, if your worker lives in a major crossroads of world travelers, you might need to "protect" him from being a perpetual host and tour guide!

Communication support is caring about your missionary and then expressing it!

It Happened This Way in Spain

I was asked to do a *Serving As Senders* Seminar for a denominational conference in Spain. I met with the mission families ahead of time. I told them I would be challenging the pastors to accept the new responsibility of member care; the denominational missions leadership was relinquishing their efforts of fulfilling the whole task by themselves. Instead, they were expecting the churches to join as major players in the process. I encouraged those missionary families to take the initiative in developing their partnership teams. They needed to work with their church leadership in designing a program that fit in with the church's means. We also discussed many of the difficulties to overcome.

The next day the seminar went really well. I had an excellent translator who was already familiar with the book, *Sirviendo al enviar Obraros* (Spanish translation of *Serving As Senders*). As I often do, even before the first break, I told them I did not want anyone coming up to me to say "what a great seminar this is." Rather, go back to your church, put these principles into practice, and after six or eight months write to me. Tell me what you are doing as a result of this seminar. I will then write back to you and say, "That was sure a great seminar!" For if no action is taken, the seminar is basically a waste of time!

Well, on the afternoon break, a brother came to me. He was that denomination's missions coordinator for a South American country. He had heard of this conference in Spain and had come specifically to invite me to come to his country. He said he didn't have to wait for six or eight months to share with me. With the flourish of a passionate Latino, he opened a large 24 x 36 inch display chart. It pictured each of the country's missionary families and pictures of the leadership. And he said, "We have developed a partnership care group for each of these families, following the principles of your book. Won't you please come and do a conference for us?"

I told him that I was not needed there. Rather, he was already doing it! I commended him for—as a denomination—taking the initiative in getting the churches reengaged in the missions process in this vital area of member care.

"Reach out and touch someone," the Bell telephone system used to say. You can still do it through soul-satisfying communication support. But the full circle of supporting your missionary is completed as you receive him back home through reentry support.

(In addition to the individual study below, see the **Group Leader's Guide** for Chapter Six beginning on page 208.)

FOR YOUR PERSONAL INVOLVEMENT

- Read one of Paul's Letters and highlight all references to personal messages and comments. You may be surprised how much his Letters dealt with personal communication, logistics and the desire to just relate with them.
- Select one of the other Letter-writers in the Bible. Identify what kinds of personal things he talked about.
- Check with the mission groups of other churches to discover what specific ideas they use in their communication support.
- Talk with your (or other) missionaries who are on home assignment. Find out from them the kinds of communication support they receive, which are appreciated the most and why.
- Review the different methods of communication suggested in this chapter. Which are you particularly interested in? Do you have the necessary equipment for that or those methods?

ACTION STEPS

By the time you have read Chapter Six, completed the

For Your Personal Involvement section and participated in a discussion group, you should ...

- Be able to decide if this is the area of support the Lord is directing you into. If so, get their email address, find out any caution in what you may say, write to that missionary God has put on your heart and press "send"!

- Prepare a form for father, mother, and children to be completed before they go, telling of their needs and wants. Be sure to include a place for their birthdays and anniversaries, types of books they like, music or study CDs they enjoy. If your missionaries are already on the field, email the form to them. When they return it, be sure to follow through regularly with at least some of their requests.

- If your worker is overseas, find out what types of things survive through the mail and what things to avoid sending. Determine costs of packages of various weights and the approximate time it takes between sending and receiving a package.

- Multiply yourself. Actively share what you are doing and look for others who might get involved.

CHAPTER 7

Reentry Support

"And they abode a long time with the disciples there."
Acts 14:28

"**M**Y FATHER WAS A career missionary. My brothers and sisters and I were born on the mission field. This was our life. Dad diligently directed a theological seminary for the whole western region of the country. Mother stood faithfully by his side. Our education was as much enhanced by watching their lives as it was by the lessons we learned in our classrooms.

"Through the years they had weathered any number of storms that assail missionaries. Each brought them to a more determined level of commitment to our Lord and to the cause of training national leadership.

"Tensions between national Christians and missionary leadership were frequent, but my dad was a peacemaker. He could walk that delicate line of cultural sensitivity. Lack of funds became so common that we all knew when to 'tighten our belts.' Discouragement over 'promising' national students who turned their backs on Christian service only toughened Dad's resolve to pour his life into others.

"But probably the most trying experience Dad and Mom faced was his arrest and uncertain life and death outcome during a military coup. With all the dramatics of a war movie, soldiers barged into our house and took Dad captive. They were sure he had 'secret contacts with the enemies of the people.'

"The coup failed. After three weeks Dad was released and resumed his work at the seminary.

"We kids are grown now. Several of us are married and back on the mission field ourselves.

"Last summer, when Dad was home, he called us all together for a family meeting. By the curtness of the invitation and the insistence on our being there, we could tell something was wrong. In a thousand years we would have never dreamed of what would take place. The meeting was short and to the point. In essence: 'Children, it is important for you to know that I am divorcing your mother. I plan to marry Sue.' Sue is younger than I am! His parting words were, 'And furthermore, I'm not even sure there is a God!'"

In the secular world of business, they are saying it: Reentry is often the hardest part of an overseas experience and it should not be ignored. There are unexpected problems in returning home. Family members who have lived in another culture need to learn how to overcome the difficulties of today's workplace, community and school environments.

In military ranks, they are saying it: Post Traumatic Stress Syndrome is debilitating thousands of our men and women returning from front lines of battle. The Pentagon has launched "Real Warriors"—a program in which service members can talk about and listen to stories of those who sought help. Yet, the suicide rate of returned veterans soars from two to four times the national average.

In the Christian community, they are saying it: Up to 50% of first-time missionaries return home early or don't return for a second term. These wounded people need to identify and process the hurt and anger of failure—to begin to build up their lives again, growing toward mental, emotional and spiritual wholeness.

In missions seminars, they are saying it: I have not taught one seminar about the acute need for reentry help without some missionary coming to me, saying, 'I thought I was weird. I couldn't tell anyone about my feelings. Thank you for letting me know that it is okay to feel a little uncomfortable in coming home.' More dramatically, just as I finished the reentry session of one seminar, a woman in the front began weeping, then uncontrollably wailing. Finally, through her tears, she screamed, 'I have been home from Indonesia for three months. Everything you just talked about—I am experiencing. Please help me!'

THE SITUATION OF REENTRY

There is an initial *shock* in returning home. Old buildings have been torn down; new ones have taken their place. A favorite park is now a freeway interchange. The environmental and political climates have changed. The school curriculum and what is taught on 200+ TV channels has changed. Grandma's rocking chair is empty. Your cross-cultural worker probably heard about some of these things as the changes happened. Now that he is home and sees them for himself, however, it really hits him hard. As with an electric shock, though, these factors are gradually absorbed and accepted.

The stress of coming home is another issue. There is a mental stretching as he is trying to incorporate new ideas and ideals gained on the field into the old—which isn't old anymore since it also is new and strangely different. *Everything* now has to be perceived through his new frame of reference.

There is a spiritual duress caused by the continual memory of the needs of a world lost in sin and what we are or aren't doing about those needs.

There is a real, internal conflict as well-meaning people gorge their newly returned missionary with rich American non-food foods. "You're so skinny; have some more!"

There are conflicting emotions, as perhaps your missionary tries to justify the new $500 wardrobe of clothes that has just been graciously given him. Days before he left the field, his national partner had been reluctant to receive a shirt from him with the words, "I have one to wear while I wash the other. A third one just isn't needed!"

Yes, the home scene with its people, places, and things—all that you represent—has changed. But more dramatically, your missionary friend has changed—socially, emotionally, mentally, physically and most of all spiritually. And because these changes happened to each of you so gradually, you yourselves are only slightly aware of them. But as you meet, the changes in each other appear drastic!

Needless to say, the longer your cross-cultural worker has been away, the more pronounced will be the culture stress in coming home.

But even short assignments can produce dramatically bold changes. A zealous Pharisee named Saul was on a mission. In that foreign land of Syria, he was riding toward Damascus. In the span of a few minutes, his entire life was changed. In a blinding light, his eyes were opened (Acts 9:1-20)!

> "Your friend has changed—most of all, spiritually."

In many situations of world need today, God can instantly open your missionary's eyes to areas of need for ministry. A short-term mission trainer reports, "For simple exposure to another culture, we have taken people across the border into Mexico and watched God stir their hearts with compassion for the lost and needy of this world in just one afternoon."

There is another factor to consider in reentry support: denial. Some workers may prepare to return home denying that they will face any stress upon reentry. Some steel themselves with the attitude that "it won't—it can't happen to me."

Denial can be suicide—emotional, spiritual, mental. And even literal, physical suicide has been the result of some missionaries' shock and stress in reentry. Your returning missionary may think, "Look how easy it was for me to adjust to my new culture on the field. What's the big deal? I'm just going home!"

Here are some possible blind spots in that statement:

1) The adaptation probably wasn't as easy or as brief as he now remembers it;

2) The months (maybe years) of anticipation before going gave him time to prepare for the adjustments;

3) The nationals of the host culture may have been accustomed to Americans and therefore knew how to help him adapt. In many cultures the people are very gentle, non-demanding and forgiving of a missionary's cultural blunders.

None of those factors will cushion his reentry as he comes home. Perhaps his unaware friends back home are innocently echoing the same words: "What's the big deal? He's just coming home!" Because many of them have not ventured beyond the comfort zones of their own world, they have no idea of what a missionary goes through in living and ministering in a second culture. Thus returning missionaries have to face the lack of interest from church people, family and friends. Many people in the home culture feel coming home is basically a non-issue.

"What's the big deal? He's just coming home!"

Awareness of the factors of reentry can prepare you to become a strongly supportive friend in the "coming back home" process.

THE CHALLENGE OF REENTRY

As a reentry support person, it is necessary for you to keep your eyes and ears open for signs of culture stress in reverse. The returning field worker is the one least prepared to handle the situation. He knows something's not right! "But what do I do?" The loneliness, the disappointment and letdown, feelings of isolation and not belonging here, the dizzying speeds of everything may find him silently crying, "Slow down! Slow down!" But things don't slow down.

You must take the initiative. You must be the "intensive care unit" for your missionary's reentry. He will face challenges of reentry in any one or more of the following areas:

1) *Physically*. We joke about jet lag: "Jet lag is the process of making you look like your passport photo!" It is a serious issue that can last for several days. Though, for his next trip, you are going to provide him with a bottle of *Oxygen Boost*, which if used properly, will eliminate (or greatly reduce) jet lag.

But the physical challenge that your returning missionary friend may experience goes beyond jet lag. If he has ministered at an elevation greatly different than the one to which he returns, adjustment time is needed. Foods may be drastically different, even affecting his digestive system. Climatic conditions, such as moving from hot to cold regions or humid to dry areas do not allow for immediate adjustment. Seasonal changes experienced by returning from the Southern Hemisphere to the Northern may give your friend a difficult adjustment. You need to help your friend (and others who observe the action) understand that it is OK to reach for a sweater in 75-degree weather when he has just returned from the hot and humid rain forest jungles of Peru to the balmy temperate zone of Southern California.

> "He reached for a sweater in 75-degree weather!"

2) *Professionally*. After the adventure of an overseas experience, going back to his old job could be very boring. Equally perplexing could be the "big-fish-in-a-little-pond" syndrome. Upon return, he suddenly becomes a small-to-medium-sized-fish in a much bigger pond! He may lament, "The light of my testimony looked so much brighter out there where it was dark!" Possibly he will sense an under-utilization of the skills and experiences he gained on the field. Or he may feel the loss of some degree

of independence as he is now under the more watchful eye of his employer. Or the feeling of being in the old rat race may begin to haunt him.

In some areas of work, a year or two away may find the old job obsolete. One woman working in computers realized this during her field training before she went to the field. Helping her through that stress before she left made reentry easier for her. In fact, when she returned, she said, "I didn't go back into computers. I am working at a nursing home. I see this as a ministry now, and the medical training I'm getting will really open up new opportunities for me to go again where laborers are needed."

On the other hand, a missionary had established a Bible School, investing nine years in teaching and administering it, and training up others to carry it forward. When he returned home, he expected encouragement from his sending church to continue in ministry. He received not even a meeting with the pastor! He went back into construction work. He is now retired. Unfortunately, the hurt lingers until today.

3) *Materially-Financially.* The America your worker is coming back to is generally much more expensive. That doesn't mean that a loaf of bread necessarily costs more. It does mean that Americans spend more money on things than do the people of the culture from which he is returning.

When your cross-cultural worker return to this, it may cause stress! When he sees a teenager go to a full closet of clothes and cry, "I don't have anything to wear!" he remembers the hours he labored over how to ask "the people back home" for a few extra dollars to feed and clothe the neighborhood kids. Or when he sees the hundreds of dollars spent on video games and remembers the plastic bags bound into a ball for the neighborhood kids to play soccer—stress!

One recently returned missionary said, "The wealth of this country is very difficult to handle; the wealth of the church is even more difficult for me to deal with."

Another missionary said, "It happened to my wife this way: A few months after our return from Mozambique, she was leisurely walking the aisles of a supermarket, choosing sale items and wisely picking them off the shelves. All of a sudden, a feeling of being overwhelmed consumed her. She began thinking, 'There are too many choices. I have to get out of here!' She left her half-full cart right in the aisle, went to the car and drove home!" These issues can appear months—even years—after a missionary returns home.

> "It's mine! It's *really* mine!"

In Brazil, due to our various economic and living conditions, personal ownership took a back seat in our minds. Upon our arrival home, I began working with a fellow who was using a new BIC felt point pen (they had not been on the market when we left). He let me use it. I commented to him how I enjoyed the feel of it and how good the writing looked.

The next day he gave me one. "Here, this is yours!" For several days, I would pause and just look at that 59¢ treasure. I would muse to myself, 'It's mine! It's really mine!'

"Ridiculous!" you might say. Yes, but this is the very level on which culture stress in reverse occurs.

Comparative wealth can begin the stress even before your missionaries leave the field. Children are susceptible as well as adults: Bill and Alice were house parents in a children's home for Wycliffe Bible Translators in the northern Philippines. Their son William had had an opportunity to spend a week in a tribal village with his dad.

Sometime after his return to the Wycliffe Center, Alice saw William looking into his clothes closet. He was crying. Knowing her own concern for how little they had compared to their lifestyle back in the States, she went to console him. After several attempts at resisting her comfort, he said, "No, Mom. I feel sad that I have so much in comparison to my new friends in the tribe."

Imagine if your friend had been working with the Dalits (250 million people who are treated like slaves and considered less valuable than animals) in India and he returns to your middle class affluence. Are you prepared to help him adjust? (Request your free copy of Gospel For Asia's book, *No Longer a Slumdog*: www.gfa.org/book to learn more about a tremendous work with these people for whom Christ died.)

4) *Culturally.* New beliefs, values, attitudes and behaviors have become a part of your returning worker. Perhaps he has adjusted to a culture with a slower pace, a more relaxed atmosphere, an emphasis on people and relationships rather than on production and results, zestier foods, a noon-hour siesta....

The cultural differences that your returning missionary may try to hold on to are innumerable. When schedules and attitudes of people here at home now don't allow for them, he feels irritation and stress!

One major expectation of most returnees is that people will be interested in their experiences: "We had been invited to their house for the evening," one returning missionary wrote. "We assumed it was to be able to share the excitement of our missionary venture. After a delicious meal during which we were able to insert a few comments, we were ushered into the family room. 'Now is our opportunity,' I thought. But as our host turned on the TV, he said, 'I was sure you would enjoy watching the NFL playoffs on our new giant-screen TV!' I was absolutely devastated! How could any game be more important or more interesting than stories of our years of service?" Both the host and the missionary had good intentions. They were just coming from very different perspectives.

What a different story is told of the Antioch church welcoming home their travel-weary pioneer missionaries: "From there they sailed back to Antioch where they had first been commended to the grace of God for the task which they had now completed. When they arrived there, they called the whole church together and rehearsed before them *all* that God had done with them, and how He had opened the door of faith to the Gentiles" (Acts 14:26-27).

They had been gone two years. To share all must have taken many sessions on many occasions. In fact, Paul was allowed to rehearse some of his stories again—four or five years later! For, Doctor Luke is the one who wrote them down, those many years later. (I have a ten-year-old story I would like to tell you ... but I will restrain myself!)

5) *Socially.* Many people place an "unholy" halo about a missionary. He is held aloof as if he is right next to God. "How can we relate with someone who has been a missionary?" they wonder. "What would we talk about?"

Or some may fear that the missionary is 'contagious'! "If I have them over for dinner, will my kids come down with some kind of disease?" Worse! "Their enthusiasm for missions might rub off on me or my spouse! My kids might 'catch' their crazy ideas!"

It might seem to returning missionaries that everyone is hurrying here and there. After spending some time here, one perceptive international observed: "In America, everyone has a watch, but no one has any time. In our country, few have watches, but everybody has time!"

Compared with much of the rest of the world, life in the United States is extremely busy. When your missionary went to the field, his old friends closed the gap that was created in their lives by his departure. Social ties may have been broken with time. Former friends—and their children—have made new friends. Once-dear families may have moved away.

If communication between the missionary and his home church has not been good or if it is a particularly large church, he may not have even been missed! One returning missionary who had spent two years of fruitful labor in Europe was greeted by his mission pastor with, "Hi, John! How was Hawaii?"

One short-term missionary, after returning from a five-week ministry, was welcomed back at church with "Bill! You've come back! We thought you had backslid!" It was a blow for the returning missionary

> "You're back! We thought you'd backslid!"

since it basically meant he wasn't being prayed for while on his mission. And if they really thought he had backslid, why weren't they out looking for him?

On the other hand, I had come home from a rather potentially dangerous trip. During the greeting time my first Sunday back, one of our prayer warriors gave me a big hug, stepped back and said, "Neal, I am sure glad you are home. This has been the hardest trip for *me* that you have ever been on!" I still rejoice in that expression of care.

There are real situations that may cause stress, but there are also imaginary ones that can be equally distressing: A family recently returned home to their church which had been kept informed about their mission. The husband said, "My best friends went sailing by, barely saying hello as if I had only been away for a long weekend. I was mortified! I was distraught!" His friends meant no harm. But rejection, whether real or imagined, can have equal consequences.

6) *Linguistically.* Your returning missionary has probably learned a second language—or at least some phrases. There are many languages of the world far more descriptive

than English. He may try to express himself in our limited vocabulary and feel inadequate. Stress! He may have "forgotten" certain English words—which may be seen as humorous or inconsequential to most of his listeners. Stress! Some of his responses might automatically come out in his second language. Stress!

Further, colloquialisms and slang have changed. Teenagers of returning families might especially feel stressed by not knowing which words are in or out—or even if "in" and "out" are in or out! When you see a puzzled look on your returning friend's face, it may be the stress of not understanding American English!

7) *Nationally, Politically.* New leadership can bring new laws. As America more and more embraces a pluralistic society, a returning missionary could experience stress, wondering under which god our one nation stands.

A visit to Iguazu Falls in southern Brazil can make the USA's Niagara Falls look like a miniature cascade! What happens to American nationalistic pride when we discover that even our English Bibles are being printed in China? Or when the mass transit systems of world-class cities make the clog and smog of our freeways a disgrace? Stress!

Having seen the other side of American foreign policies, your missionary's political outlook on this country may be affected. Possibly your returning worker found the government of his host country more to his liking. Americans who live abroad sometimes feel that a socialized government offers more security to its citizens than does the free enterprise of the US. As a returned worker simply reads a Yahoo news editorial about issues now facing his own society, he may be irritated with stress! And that is when you as a reentry support "specialist" (really, just a friend) need to have your eyes and ears open! You are needed to ask a few gentle, interested questions to encourage him to talk more—to process the good and the not-so-good of his ministry experience. This will help him more easily see the good and the not-so-good of his home culture in perspective.

8) **Educationally.** The formal and informal educational standards of the world vary. Missionary children may have for years been educated by home schooling or at a boarding school away from their parents. When the kids now have to go to a large public school, parents can understandably be concerned. The kids themselves can feel they are in a potentially devastating situation educationally as well as socially.

One girl, returning from the field to spend her seventh grade in a US school, described her first day: "We circled the monstrous wood and brick building. We surged forward, carried irresistibly toward its mouth. We stopped momentarily at its gaping door.... I was now in the monster's throat. I felt a downward, sinking feeling. I was being swallowed! The noise was like thunder.... I was alone in the blackness of that nightmare."

Actually, that description could fit what your returning missionaries and their children each might sense during the weeks and months of reentry.

9) **Spiritually.** Your returning cross-cultural worker's life has concentrated on the salvation and discipling of the nations. He has sensed the very heartbeat of God pounding in his breast: "God is not willing that any perish, but that all come to repentance" (2 Peter 3:9). He has become disentangled with the affairs of this world "that he may please the One who has called him to be His soldier" (2 Timothy 2:4). He remembers the cry of the widow, the orphan, the lost and dying.

And now in bold, stark contrast, the demands of what is (or appears to be) a "godless Christian" society surround him with stress. He is enjoying the pleasures of new conveniences at home in America, yet even that enjoyment can create feelings of bewilderment, anger, guilt and condemnation. The hurt is not only for himself; it is also for the hundreds of people he left back in his adopted country who need food and care and Bibles and Christian music and Bible studies and the many other blessings too easily taken for granted in America.

Each of these areas—from physical to spiritual factors—is a stress point needing your reentry support.

REENTRY BEHAVIOR PATTERNS

There are at least five patterns of return behavior that could show up in your missionary friend. Four of them are dangerous. You want to be alert to their symptoms and help your friend process his feelings, working toward the expression of the fifth pattern. That is the one you want to facilitate. And by focusing on it, your friend will be less likely to fall into one of the others.

1) *Alienation.* The cross-cultural worker comes home. His attitude of "I'm just going home!" has left him unprepared for what he is facing. He begins feeling very negative about his home culture. Not knowing how to handle what he sees and feels, he begins withdrawing.

   He makes excuses rather than meeting people. "I don't have my PowerPoint together yet," he says. So he can't share with the home fellowship group. "The crowd at the baseball game would be too noisy," he argues. Three weeks later he is still "suffering from jet lag." These are the types of symptoms you must be on the lookout for. They may be shallow pretexts to hide his inner feelings.

   He might internalize these feelings and sink further into this pattern of alienation. He may feel there is no one to talk to, no one who could possibly understand, no one to help him process his thoughts.

   You can pull him out of that tailspin by inviting him to your home. Just the two of you—or three—is a small, safe number. Or visit some of his favorite spots together—a park, a beach, a restaurant. If he refuses all of this, get desperate! Just show up at his doorstep and insist on some fellowship! Get him talking about anything, just so he begins verbalizing his thoughts.

Here are some simple, yet effective conversation starters:

- What was the most rewarding, surprising, scariest, funniest thing that happened?
- What really stretched you culturally? spiritually?
- What is one new thing God showed you about Himself? about yourself?

2) *Condemnation.* This person is also negative about his home culture. The areas of challenge seem to be overwhelming. He didn't realize people would be so unthinking—so uninterested in anything that looked beyond their "little world". He can't understand why his pastor has no time for him. How could people be so— unChristian? The pressure of his judgmental attitude increases, and he becomes explosive. Everyone he sees knows within minutes how inferior and lacking in spiritual gifts they are—so he thinks—because they are not involved in missions. He begins to condemn and criticize everything from the church pews to Mrs. O'Toole's new hairstyle.

> "Don't let his judgmental attitude put you on the defensive."

Since he is so forcefully verbalizing his criticisms, it may cause you to become defensive. Don't let it! Remember, this is *his* problem. Let him talk to you. Help him deal with these issues before he develops a root of bitterness (Hebrews 12:15). He, too, needs to process all of his frustrations in the safe environment of a close friendship. Don't wait until he feels he must unload in the middle of the pastor's Sunday sermon.

It was time to give the leased orphan houses back to the owner. Rather than leasing again, Rose thought to purchase some land—enough for a home for her 100 children, a piggery and a rice field. To accomplish this would only cost $50,000. A letter was sent home and distributed. No response! She came home. To her utter dismay, the people of her sending church were arguing over one color or another for new carpet in the sanctuary that didn't even need new carpet! Cost: $30,000! It was time for some gentle, but firm intervention by her reentry support friends. What could have become a wild scene of condemnation became, for her, a lesson in priorities. (Learn more about this tremendous ministry at www.mmfthailand.org.)

3) *Reversion.* This person takes a hop, skip and a jump off the plane only to discover people aren't hopping, skipping and jumping any more. Yet he keeps trying to deny that any vital changes took place in him while he was gone, or in you who stayed home. He keeps trying to fit in to what was before but no longer is.

   This person is likely to jump right into whatever task is put before him. And his unaware friends play right into this dilemma: "So glad you're back! We need a teacher for the sixth grade class!" "Great! When do I start?" Usher? "Yes, I will!" Lead worship on Wednesday night? "Sure!"

   He will wake up one morning doubting his sanity. He has moved into the fast lane of American Christianity without allowing himself time to process the incredible changes his body, soul and spirit are experiencing.

4) *The Ultimate Escape.* Alienation, condemnation or reversion could lead your cross-cultural worker into a devastating scenario of the ultimate escape of suicide— emotional, mental, spiritual, and yes, even physical.

   The missionary went out to live and minister in a second culture. He had a good experience. Language was learned.

Relationships were nurtured. Souls were saved. The church was strengthened.

He returns. He is not prepared for the changes at home. He tries to cope. He internalizes all his frustrations. Alienation whispers, "Nobody cares or understands. Forget them!" He argues with himself, "No, I have to get out and share a vision for the world among the church people." "But they are so ungodly," Condemnation thunders. "This isn't getting me anywhere," he yells back at himself. Reversion reasons, "Okay, let's just forget it. I was there. You were here. We're back together. No big deal!"

The whirlwind of emotions leaves him broken. He backs out of life—spiritually, mentally, emotionally, or finds the ultimate escape his only alternative: physical suicide!

If you see your returning friend falling into any one of these four behavior patterns, your help is needed!

The most vital immediate help you can give is to listen! Take the time to hear his heart, to share his experiences, to care about his feelings and burdens, to see his pictures, to be there when he needs someone to talk and laugh and cry with. Learn to ask sensitive, even probing questions. Your goal is to help your friend process his missionary experiences, keeping in perspective what went well with what went not so well.

The gala reunion parties are fine. But what about at three in the morning: You're awakened by the phone. At first you don't hear anyone on the line. Then you hear someone let out a deep groan. "John, is that you?" There's only a hardly distinguishable, "Yes." You say, "I'll be right over!"

Let him say anything in the confidence of your friendship. Don't interject, "I know, yes, I understand. You just gotta' toughen up." You probably don't understand! Just let him talk. Encourage him to keep talking by asking leading questions to explain something he has referred to. Ask often, "And how did you feel when that happened?" Affirm with "That must have been tough/terrifying/exciting/etc." (Lady readers, you would *not* respond to that phone call. Likewise, men, if that were a lady on the phone, you would not "be right over!")

Because you have been sensitive to your friend's reentry needs, you have helped him avoid these negative behavior patterns. Therefore, you can help him focus on a fifth return behavior pattern—the only healthy one: Integration. It bears repeating: By initially focusing on integration, the others are more likely to be avoided.

5) *Integration.* Helping your missionary integrate takes place on two levels: Immediate and long-range.

The Immediate

a) Be sure your workers are welcomed and picked up at the airport. Don't overwhelm them with half the church being there, but a good-sized group who will say, "We're glad you're home!" One church welcoming party came to the airport two days after the missionary had come home. Fortunately his parents had confirmed the correct day of his arrival and were there to meet him!

b) Have a place for them to stay. "And [Paul and Barnabas] abode with them for a long time" (Acts 14:28)! It is noteworthy that of the twelve Greek words we translate "abide," the one used here is defined as "to wear through by rubbing; to rub away!" In other words, their stay with the disciples in Antioch was of such a duration that all strangeness of relationship was "rubbed away!" When you abide with someone, you know where the extra light bulbs are stored. You aren't just camped out in the front hallway. Whether it is with friends, family, or in a place of their own, be sure to check with your missionaries before they return. Let them be prepared for the accommodations you are providing for them.

As a church recently brought home their first missionary

family, the missions pastor said, "The washer and dryer are hooked up. The utilities are on, the refrigerator is stocked and the telephone is in service. I think we're ready!"

c) Have an immediate means of transportation for them—a borrowed car or a dependable, inexpensive one that can be sold when they return to the field.

> "Initially focus on integration."

One returning woman said, "Not only did they have a comfortable, dependable car available for my three months home, but a gas credit card for my use!" It is important that returning missionaries have some independence and the freedom to be mobile.

d) Provide meals for the first few days. Invite them over; bring food in; have their home stocked with some basic food supplies—and maybe a few treats. Take them out to their favorite restaurant. Be sensitive. Don't make it difficult for them to say "No." Some missionaries have said, "I can hardly wait to get back to the field. I won't have to eat so much!"

e) Take them shopping. They may not know what styles are fashionable. And they can look conspicuously out of place without even knowing it! Care must be taken here also, for your friend may have learned to dress more conservatively and manage with fewer clothes.

f) Perhaps they had complete medical check-ups just before leaving the field. If not, ask them if they would appreciate your making arrangements for doctor, dental and eye care visits—free or discounted or paid for by you or the church!

g) After an appropriate few days, have a get-together—perhaps a potluck dinner—so they can meet more people in a shorter time. A ladies' tea is great for the women to catch up and again feel a part of things. But again, be sensitive. They may want to spend most of their time alone for the first week or so.

One church wisely made arrangements for their missionary family to spend two weeks in a home in Hawaii, just to "regroup" as a family, before returning to the States.

h) Remember the children! It can so easily be thought that only Dad and Mom are the missionaries, what could the "kids" possibly need? They're young. They can adjust. No! Each is an individual; each has personal needs. Yes, they can adjust as their individual needs are considered and attended to.

One family had ministered in Asia for many years. Their oldest son, John, had graduated well from the mission school. Dad brought him home to get him set up in college. Letters came back about how well he was doing. A year later, Mother brought their daughter home (she had graduated with honors) to get set up in college. Letters came back that "things" weren't going so well. "John is doing so well. I'm sure you will, too, honey. Just give things time to work out." Six months later the daughter committed suicide! If you had been living near that college, would you have been available and willing to help?

Long Range Interaction

Help returned missionaries to *slowly* integrate their new identity and lifestyle into their new environment. They have the opportunity and challenge to be positive change agents—people who can purposefully help all of you back home to see the world more and more from God's perspective. Be open to their new ideas and ways of doing things.

Paul and Barnabas, on their arrival in Antioch, were given the opportunity to "call the Church together and report to them all that God had done with them and how He had opened the door of faith to the Gentiles" (Acts 14:27). You want to provide an environment for your missionary friend to debrief on both levels: What God has done with them and how He has "opened the door of faith ..." in whatever ministry he was engaged.

Look for creative ways to help your missionary introduce global perspectives to your friends. What groups of people could you interest in hearing his report: Sunday service congregations? Sunday school classes? Home fellowships? Prayer groups? Public and private schools? Other churches' groups? Christian radio or TV? Secular radio or TV? A newspaper article? Is his story worth writing a book about? Could you provide his story with video clips on a business card DVD for him to distribute as he travels? Arranging meetings for him with a variety of groups forces him to process the good and not-so-good of his experiences as he prepares for each new venue. This is good. It helps him keep everything in perspective as he readjusts to his home culture.

Also have a keen, listening ear to hear what God has done in his life. Allow him to say those things that can't be said publicly. Help him sort through those private issues that can so easily become the roots of bitterness.

Scripture further says of Paul and Barnabas that they stayed in Antioch for some time, teaching and preaching the Word of the Lord (Acts 15:35). In other words, the time came when they picked up the ministry they had been involved in before going. In its time—if they are not returning to the field—taking up a ministry in the church would be a goal for your cross-cultural workers. This might possibly be in their area of previous ministry. But it is also possible that with their cross-cultural ministry experience, they would now be suited to further develop your church's involvement with internationals who live among you. Or to train new missionary recruits. Or to develop the many aspects of strong sending teams.

PERSONALIZING REENTRY SUPPORT

There may be special reentry concerns for various members of the family:

1) Husbands can use help.

As a family returns from the field, there are pressures and anxious feelings of responsibility on the husband as provider. Financial support may have dropped off because they aren't on the field now, yet expenses are probably higher here at home.

Take the initiative in talking about money. Maybe you can help financially, maybe not. But you have helped by bringing the subject "out of the closet." Let him verbalize his family's needs. Even that may help to sort out priorities. And, then again, it might bring a totally new, Holy Spirit-inspired solution.

Go easy on this, but the time will come to help him talk about future plans. "What livelihood are you going to pursue?" "Are you planning to go back for more schooling?" "Back to the field?" "Back to your previous employment?"

Remember, a "listening ear" is one that is "hearing" all that is being said, all that is not being said, as well as the non-verbal messages that are being communicated.

2) Behind every good man is a great wife!

On the field she probably played a much more active role in ministry than she will now. Be sure to allow opportunities for her to share. If this is not appropriate in your public gatherings, provide occasions in your living room. Often the wife in the missionary team bore enormous pressures in the balance of ministry and family affairs, and her needs to share are equally valid.

She is pleased with the fully carpeted, three-bedroom, two-bath house the church rented for them. But she is at a loss as to how she is going to keep it clean! More often than not on the field she had a maid who had helped even with the cooking!

Help her ease back into the skills of homemaking. Be willing to help her with it for a time.

I had just completed a Wednesday evening lesson on reentry care with a congregation, which was just sending out their first missionary family. A woman approached me, uncontrollably crying. I held her hands, crying with her, sensing some deep issue. When she could speak through her tears she said, "I just want to go back. All I want to do is go back!"

She had been raised on the mission field. When she was eighteen, the family came home. Her reentry "care" consisted of this statement from her father: "You're in America now. Live like an American!"

Now, twenty years later, she is married and has three children. Her heart cry is, "I want to go back!" After many more tears and some encouraging words, I said, "You are fortunate that you never had the opportunity to go back." She was most surprised at that. For the last 20 years, she thought it would have helped her. She asked why I thought she should not go back.

The image she had built up in her mind had probably never existed, but for sure it didn't now. Without anything else to hold on to, this dream was helping her maintain. If she had gone back and seen that the dream was not there, there is no telling what she would have done.

3) Missionary kids are ordinary kids.

Born to American parents but raised in Japan, Zaire, Cairo or Hong Kong, missionary kids (MKs) often don't know where they fit! America is their homeland, but it usually isn't their home.

It was my privilege to help one seventeen-year-old sort through this issue: His mother was Canadian. His father held USA citizenship, but this youth had been born and raised in Brazil. He was Brazilian. He had passports for all three, but as an adult (at eighteen) he would have to give up one identity. Does he deny his mother's homeland? his father's? his own?

A 14-year-old MK, after returning to the field from a year back in the US, wrote a ninth-grade essay titled,

What I Would Like to Tell the People Back Home.

I want to answer a few questions I have been asked: No! We don't live in mud huts. No! We don't eat "foreign" food. It is very natural. MKs are not perfect. We're human and have faults and virtues like everybody else. When you subconsciously or otherwise treat us like we should be perfect, we get chewed out by you (who have no right at all) and then by our parents (who know better).

No! All MKs are not super brats. Those few who might act like it on furlough are probably trying to hide the culture shock they are going through. No! Just because you're an MK doesn't mean you know your Bible any better than anyone else. All the time when we were on furlough, I was asked to quote Scripture or find something in the Bible I had never heard of. People were shocked and whispered behind their hands.

No! MKs don't go around barefoot and in rags. Mrs. X had seen a picture of me in a paint-spotted tee-shirt and cutoffs and assumed I didn't have anything better to wear.

Please send money! The money sent to missionaries is never enough! Even though it often appears my folks aren't doing anything, they are! And our national friends will tell you so!

How can you support a returning MK? You will use all the tenderness and understanding and tact and wisdom and patience you would employ in being a reentry support person for Mom or Dad.

4) Single and satisfied!

This phrase (the title and subject of a book) might remind senders that singles need special reentry support, too. Few married people understand single ministry workers' needs of being cared for. And few married couples realize the unintentional insensitivity and hurt hurled at single adults in even Christian circles.

Sometimes reentry is harder for a single. At least family members have each other to talk with. Loneliness, perplexities, inability to cope with modern single relationships and the desire to get on with life can throw unmarried returned missionaries into quagmires of alienation and depression. You need to be there to draw them out! Be there to listen and serve as their "intensive care unit" (though, again, men with men; women with women).

We are the Body of Christ. We are a community of believers. We really do need each other. May God challenge you to become part of a reentry support team who are serving as senders!

It Happened This Way in Washington

A "church" was crying. "What did we do wrong? Why didn't we see this coming?"

A young wife and her husband had recently returned from a very difficult mission assignment. The church observed them having little fights, but they didn't know what to do. The church observed them always getting sick, but they didn't know what to do. Then the church decided, "We know what to do. We'll leave them alone. We know they love each other. We're sure they will work it out."

The couple didn't know what to do. One evening as they were getting ready for church, the wife said, "Honey, I don't feel well. You go ahead. I need to stay home." Not knowing what to do, she committed suicide.

The northwest regional office of their agency knew nothing of the struggles this couple was experiencing. The national director of member care for that organization didn't know what to do. He was in denial. He said, "That sort of thing doesn't happen!" just three months after it happened. All involved were devastated by her death. Nobody had known what to do!

It clearly became a "wake-up" call to the church and the regional office.

Hank, working in that Northwest agency office, decided to make a commitment to do all he could to not allow this to happen again. I happened to be in the area at the time, doing seminars on Member Care. Hank called me: "Would you be willing to do an eight-minute interview on the importance of reentry care?" Hank went into high gear! He was able to assign another person to this task. Bill interviewed me on video and also created a cartoon character presentation of the concepts of *Serving as Senders*. He was now ready for action.

When a missionary family was one year from returning home, he would contact them, asking for permission to talk with their home church pastor: "I have some resources that will help them help you to have a good return home."

Church identified and permission granted, Bill called the pastor. "I understand you have a missionary family coming home in about nine months. We have some resources to share with you to help you help them experience a good reentry. I have a brief DVD I would like to show you on the importance of reentry for a missionary." I am sure there were other pleasantries shared, but basically Bill wanted an entrance to that church to get them educated and involved in this part of the missions process.

(He had the suicide clearly in his mind to motivate him.)

Appointment set, Bill visited with the pastor. He showed the interview and gave him a copy of the book. "Now, Pastor," Bill said, "I know you are busy with many responsibilities. But I am sure you have a missions committee or a group of this missionary's friends who would be willing to help them on their reentry. May I talk with them about this critical, but often neglected, time in the life of a missionary?"

Again, permission granted, Bill came back to meet with this group. He shared his cartoon presentation, answered questions and gave them an opportunity to purchase copies of the book. They did.

Up to this point it is a great story. For several years, we were providing that agency with cases of *Serving As Senders*. But, one day, I realized the orders had stopped. I called Hank. "What's up?" I asked. "Are all the churches in your region fully functioning in their care of missionaries?"

His next words are some of the saddest I have ever heard: "No, Neal. Bill retired. I was moved to another department. I no longer have any say in the area of member care. And it will probably take another suicide for them to reinstate that program!"

> *Subsequent to the writing of* Serving As Senders, *I have had numerous opportunities to share these principles of missionary care. Soon I became aware that reentry care was the least understood of the six areas.*
>
> *Thus, I embarked on the task of writing a book specifically dealing with care at this most critical time in the life of a missionary:* The Reentry Team: Caring For Your Returning Missionaries. *In Section I, I present the Biblical model and then the human dilemma that makes it so difficult to follow that so simply stated five-step model. Section II contains seventy stories written by returned missionaries. Each one is followed by a bit of commentary and action steps to help the reader avoid the pitfalls of the negative experiences and emulate the successes of the positive stories (www.eri.org).*

Though the NASA Space Shuttle program has been retired, watching those "big birds" land should still be in your memory. But before we can see them in the sky, there is a critical maneuver the pilot must make. He has to "hit" the earth's atmosphere at the precise angle. Too shallow of an angle will have him bouncing off into outer space. Too sharp of an angle will have that ship burning up.

It is exactly the same with a returning missionary. You need to be there for him to bring him back into his home culture at "just the right angle." Not too shallow: "Oh, you're back. How was your trip?" Not too sharp: "Oh, you're back. We thought you had backslid!"

This then is the full circle of support you can offer to your cross-cultural worker as you express your love and concern for him while he is preparing to go, while he is on the field and when he returns home.

(In addition to the individual study below, see the **Group Leader's Guide** for Chapter Seven beginning on page 210.)

For Your Personal Involvement

- Though this aspect of missions life had been long neglected, articles now abound on the subject. From various missionary journals, collect and read as much as you can about reentry. Realize that though material is now more available, few are yet aggressively engaging themselves in this most difficult time in the life of a missionary.

- Talk with missionaries who are on home assignment or those who have returned more permanently about the challenge of reentry. But be prepared for some tears! Many missionaries, unless they have had a good reentry support team, have a lot of bottled-up emotions!

- As you listen to these people, try to identify symptoms of the first four reentry behavior patterns.

- Write. to the mission agencies of your cross-cultural workers. Ask them for the materials and useful ideas they recommend to help bring missionaries home.

- Write to other mission agencies and ask them for their materials and procedures. Learn all you can about this needy area of missionary support.

ACTION STEPS

By the time you have read Chapter Seven, completed the *For Your Personal Involvement* section and participated in a discussion group, you should ...

- Be able to decide if this is the area of support the Lord is directing you into.

- If it is, write to the missionary God has placed on your heart. Ask him if this is okay with him. Find out if there are others who have made this commitment to him. Begin networking responsibilities with the others.

- Four months before your cross-cultural worker comes home, send him material collected on reentry that will help him prepare for his major transition.

- Purchase *The Reentry Team: Caring For Your Returning Missionaries*. Read and apply it.

- Multiply yourself. Share with others the material you collect about this most neglected area of missionary support. Be willing to train them. A good reentry doesn't "just happen!" Enlist many in this vital ministry.

CHAPTER 8

Your Part in the Big Picture

"Be strong and very courageous that you may do it!"
Joshua 1:9

"I RETURNED TO the major city, having just completed two successful weeks of training sessions in the back country. Eager students searched their Bibles and took notes for seven hours a day. We had returned a day early, so my reserved hotel room was not yet ready for me. No problem—I could go to the business center to check my emails. It was a very small room with a clerk's desk and two computer terminals. I paid the fee and opened an email from my partner who was still in another country. He said it was too 'hot' to conduct the training in this city so I needed to get on a flight first thing in the morning. He gave me the name and number of the person who would pick me up. I was thanking the Lord that I had come in a day earlier than expected. Had I not come, I would have missed connecting with him in that new location.

"While in that thankful mood, I realized the attendant had left the room. Strange, I thought. Then I began smelling an unusual smell. I looked under my table...over in the corner... under the attendant's desk. Nothing. Then it struck me: I was the smell! I hadn't had a shower for two weeks. For some reason, in the backcountry, they think that if you soak your feet in scalding hot water each night before going to bed, you are clean. Yes, you all sit on the porch, talking together and soaking your feet. And then, 'Good night!'

"Another friend helped me get on the correct flight the next morning. (Yes, I had taken a long, hot shower!) I arrived safely. However, there were no pay phones, nor did I have a cell phone. I looked around. 'Here comes a gentleman. I am sure he speaks English and will let me use his phone. Just one quick call, please.'

"I entered the number. The lady answered, 'No, I will not pick you up.' She gave me the name and number of another person. I had to ask the man to let me make another call. His taxi was waiting, but I had the phone. (Possession is nine-tenths of the law, isn't it?) I called. 'A van will be there in twenty minutes,' I was told. Soon my partner arrived. We waited.

"One hour and twenty minutes later, a van with black tint on all side and back windows, stopped. A window rolled down. A door opened. A voice from that interior blackness said, 'Get in.' We did. Only after we were down the road some distance did they introduce themselves in broken English. Our one or two words in their language could say no more than 'hello' and 'thank you!'

"We traveled in silence along a highway, then left onto a dirt road. We made a right turn some miles later onto a highway, zigzagging in generally one direction to a yet unknown destination.

"Next we left the highway onto a paved boulevard. The van slowed, turned off its lights and stopped. A voice in the dark said, 'Get out here. Hide behind those bushes. Another van will come from the opposite direction. Its lights will be off. Get into that van.' And they left!

"For men, bushes can easily become a relief station. Thus relieved, we waited. And there it came—another van from the opposite direction, with its lights off. A window rolled down and a voice from that interior darkness said, 'Get in!' And we did.

"Back on the highway, we zigzagged through the night countryside. Through villages, and now more narrow roads— some with drying crops covering half the width of the road. Then we traveled on dirt roads. The van 'bottomed out' a few times, but kept going.

"Then we heard an excited conversation on a cell phone. We approached a high, solid corrugated-iron double gate. The gates opened at the sound of the van. We drove in, then stayed in the van until the gates closed. As we got out, we were greeted by fifty pastors waiting to hear the Biblical principles of caring for the missionaries they were sending out to Middle Eastern countries.

"A feast awaited us. No matter that it was midnight! Nor did it matter that the living quarters of this compound were the resting places for a cow, a sheep, several pigs and numerous chickens! A good night's sleep and we were ready to share.

"Little did it matter to anyone that my young lady translator was wearing a sweatshirt with a playboy bunny brazened across the front. Only our culture from the West (or in the metropolitan areas of this country) would know the significance of that symbol. Eager hearts were here to learn from the Word of God.

"The week passed only too quickly. The iron gates opened into the night and we were on our way to another village area deemed safe enough for a couple of Western travelers."

"Be strong and courageous!" Why is it so crucial that you and your fellowship be strong and courageous to serve as senders? Because God is orchestrating a concert of global activity in our times in which tens of thousands of new missionaries are going to every people, tribe, tongue and nation. And every goer needs a solid team of senders. You and your church could identify and send and care for teachers to countries like this one, preparing some of those nationals to go and some to serve as senders.

A New Harvest Force

"The harvest is great; the laborers are few."

Luke 10:2

Worldwide, the harvest team is growing—particularly in the Two-Thirds World. (Two-Thirds World describes two-thirds of the world's population living on two-thirds of the earth's surface. And these countries now form more than two-thirds of the global Body of Christ.) Mission is now from everywhere to everywhere:

- A church in Mongolia was birthed in 1990. Within five years they sent their first two missionaries to India. Soon, several Mongolian congregations were sending missionaries into China, and around the globe on Operation Mobilization's Doulos and Logos, their floating evangelistic bookstores. Now the Church of hundreds of congregations in Mongolia continues to send workers into His harvest fields. (OM's lead vessel is now Logos Hope. Keep up with this fabulous ministry at www.omships.org.)

- One of Christendom's most unique missionary teams is a *Filipino* couple sent under a *Singapore* mission agency, supported by *Indonesian* churches to minister to Indians in *Paraguay*, South America.

- In 2005, the Nigerian Church through NEMA launched a Vision 50:15 strategy to aggressively send out 50,000 missionaries by the year 2020. The project seeks to include the entirety of North Africa and the Arabian Peninsula until the Gospel gets back to where it came from—Jerusalem. It is their desire to meet the Chinese there as the massive Church in China has also launched an initiative to see the Gospel sweep across the Middle Eastern countries, reaching to Jerusalem. The NEMA Executive Director stated: "Hundreds of churches have adopted the vision. Whole denominations have established weekly prayer for each of the eighteen nations we have entered. Many have adapted the book, *Serving As Senders*, as a manual for their members to provide appropriate support for their missionaries. Our first martyr was gunned down in 2010." (www.nematoday.org)

- Though the challenge for the Nigerian Church is daunting, as they "advance on their knees" through Muslim and animistic territory, the task looming before the Chinese Church is even greater. Five thousand people groups in fifty countries span the region between China and Jerusalem. These lands also hold a trio of spiritual strongholds: Hinduism, Buddhism and Islam.

The *Back to Jerusalem Movement* had its beginnings in the 1940s. Due to severe persecution in the 1950s, it went underground for many decades. However, today hundreds of Chinese families are relocating to unreached regions of China, planting new congregations. Church leaders are training and sending additional thousands west, believing God has given them the commission to complete the full circle of the Gospel around the globe. (www.backtojerusalem.com)

> "Our first martyr was gunned down in 2010."

- Korean churches, with a God-inspired zeal, continue to send missionaries to some of the hardest-to-evangelize corners of the world. Korea is the first non-Western nation to deploy such large numbers of missionaries. They are second only to the United States in the number they have on the field. Realize that less than one hundred fifty years ago, Koreans beheaded believers in Christ.

- An Armenian, whose Christian family had escaped from the Ottoman Empire three generations ago, was born in Nineveh, Iraq. In 1990, he found himself fighting for Saddam Hussein in Kuwait. He woke up one morning to realize that unless he got out of there, he would be killed. He *walked* 1500 miles to Turkey! He was shot at twice. At several borders, he was almost captured. He was able to receive political asylum through Turkey and he went to Sweden. He set up a business that became quite successful.

While in Malaysia, attending a conference related to his business, he vacationed briefly in Phuket. Walking along the ocean one day, his heart was stirred with compassion for the ladies who were parading their bodies for sale. He went home. His church could not envision a ministry to prostitutes. Garnering the support of several home groups, he returned to Malaysia. He and his wife (a woman whom he rescued from the "business") continue to minister among these people.

> *"A missionary from Nineveh!"*

- The Latin American Church as a whole has been awakened over the last decades to their responsibility to the world harvest. A number of years ago, I was asked to come to Chile. At the time, the Church represented between 18-20% of the population, a significant number. Yet church leaders were still standing at the door with their "hands out" when missionaries came, asking them to bring personnel, money and equipment. My assignment was to travel to five major speaking centers. The message they asked me to give: "It is time for you, pastors, to stop asking for help and start lifting up your eyes to the fields of the world." Now, not only from Chile, but also from Brazil, Columbia and other Latin American nations, hundreds are responding to the call to go. Many are going to the Muslim world.

- A director of one Latin American ministry said it this way:

  "Reaching Muslims has been difficult for many traditional European and North American missionaries. Their blond, Caucasian looks, their cultural differences and their mission style have often been more of a hindrance than help.

"Enter a new wave of modern missionaries, dark-skinned, soccer-loving Latin Americans who can more easily move among North African people and share an affinity with them and their culture. For historic and cultural reasons there are many similarities between Arab and Latin American cultures. For example, the way we use time, and our concept of friendship. In addition, we have been colonized just like the Arabs. They also don't feel threatened by a Latin; they don't think that he is a spy."

- A Brazilian brother enlarges on this new Harvest Force. Drawing on history, he talks about the coming of the "Third Church" of the third world in the Third Millennium. The "first church" was in the Mediterranean region led by Christ's early century followers. The "second church" was the development of the Western European and North American Church. While Christianity in much of North America and Europe stagnates, vibrant new churches are taking root around the globe. Since the 1970s, the emergence of the "third church" among countries of the Southern Hemisphere (Latin America, Africa, Asia and Oceania) have been increasingly providing the next generation of cross-cultural workers. (Google *Unleashing the Brazilian Evangelical Missionary Force.*)

A North American reader, at this point could say, "Good, the opportunity for my involvement is past. I hand the 'Torch' to the Third Church of the third world." Not so, says the Scripture! Just because God is raising up new believers who are hearing the Voice of their Master, "Go! Preach! Go! Teach!", the North American Church—more personally, you, the reader—cannot deny His clarion call to all true believers: some to go; some to serve as senders.

A few examples:

A Western missionary, who had learned how to relate with Muslims, went to Georgia (not USA) to train local Christian leaders to do summer camps for Muslim children. Impressionable and eager to understand purpose in life, a nine-year-old chose to sit and read about Jesus (because her parents would not have allowed her to have that book in their home) rather than play games with the others.

A Western missionary, who had worked with Latin American Christians, now lives in Spain where he is giving advanced training to Latinos crossing into North Africa. He comments: "Latinos are tough! They have paid a high price, showing a deep commitment to the Lord, passionate love for the lost, and admirable perseverance under difficult circumstances."

A Western missionary, who has a grasp on the basic principles of spiritual warfare, goes to Asian, European and Latin American countries to help prepare field workers being sent out from those countries.

> "There are still places of ministry for Western missionaries."

A Western missionary, who has a heart for the Bibleless peoples, went to Papua New Guinea to train nationals in Bible translation.

A Western missionary, who had prepared himself and his family, goes to the Bushmen of the Kalahari to lead to Christ those from this people group who will join in the singing of praise unto our King.

A Western missionary, maybe one you know, is developing a partnership team. And he is looking for *you*! But regardless of how many (from the East, West, North or South) commit to missions in the 21st Century, this new harvest force won't go (or worse, will go and not be as effective) unless they are sent.

In secular war, there is an acknowledged ratio of support personnel to frontline soldiers. In World War II, the military ratio was generally 15 to one. In more recent conflicts, that ratio was expanded to 50 support workers per frontline soldier.

Spiritual warfare, which encompasses all true missionary work, demands no less an emphasis on support personnel. In the 1700s, the Moravians of Central Europe enlisted four senders for

each goer. In the Student Volunteer Movement, a massive army
of 20,000 frontline missionaries was sent out. But in that same
God-inspired movement, there were 80,000 committed to care
for those who went. In 2004, at the first Guatemala National
Missions Conference, hundreds stepped forward to respond to
the call to go. A greater number, remaining in the audience,
stood and moved forward to declare their willingness to serve
as senders. Since the 21st-century harvest force is growing by
thousands of new missionaries, the sending force must grow
proportionately by tens of thousands.

Look What God Is Doing in His Harvest Field Today

"Look among the nations and watch. Be utterly astounded!
For I will do a work in your day which you would not
believe, though it were told you."
Habakkuk 1:5

To understand the significance of a sending ministry, we
need to see how it fits into the big picture of what God is doing.
The message of the Gospel never changes, but the "all things
to all men so that by all means…" (I Corinthians 9:22) does
change. For example, the following factors are affecting the
methods God is using to reap a 21st-century harvest:

- Restricted-access countries are increasing in number.
  This requires using more creative ways to gain entrance
  to that country. For instance, a Filipina taught English
  at a university. The program was structured so that she
  followed her students through their four years. Due to her
  witness, when the 34 students graduated, 27 were true
  followers of Jesus. Some four years later, she returned to
  visit several of them. One is now leading a group of 20
  single business people. Another is teaching University
  students. Another has opened a club for mothers, where
  they are learning parenting and family relationship skills,
  to stem the tide of divorce that is sweeping that country.
  These nationals are now using these means to reach and
  disciple others. (www.missionfinder.org/tesol.html)

- Business As Mission has become a viable option. Timothy, born to aristocracy, lost everything but his life in the collapse of his country. When released from prison, he found a job loading boxes at a warehouse. His entrepreneurial skills, using Business As Mission principles, have transformed not only his life, but for that of a large segment of his once decimated tribe. (www.mybusiness-mymission.com)

- A commodities trader on the New York Stock Exchange found that he was able to use his years of experience to make a difference with small businesses in Ecuador. He says that integrating his faith and passion for business will only continue. (www.businessasmission.com)

- Finishers Project is a service that helps adult Christians discover short-term, part-time, or second-career ministry opportunities. The president of Finishers Project says, "The fact that there are 78 million Boomers in the United States looking for ways to invest their experience and resources to make a difference, has not caught God by surprise. He has been preparing a unique generation for significant Kingdom expansion." A "twice-retired, still on fire" pharmaceutical manufacturer, at age 70 returned to seminary for his MA in Religion, to prepare him for ministry "until He comes." (www.finishers.org)

- A ministry in Egypt is filming simultaneously in four studios daily. They send the teachings to Europe, where they are beamed back to the Middle East. Follow up has a whole staff of people answering questions and sending out literature.

- A pastor in Turkey has an Internet ministry, developing a relationship with hundreds of Muslims who are interested in Isa (Jesus).

- Foundational to every Church Planting Movement (CPM) are intentional methods and strategies that have captured the imagination and drive of hundreds of networking missionaries around the globe. They follow a Biblical model of leaving culturally-relevant, reproducing churches, allowing them to move on to another location. (www. churchplantingmovements.com) Watchman Nee said that missionaries, at best, should see themselves as scaffolding. When the church is built up (not referring to the building, but the people), the "scaffolding" should come down, be packed up on a truck and moved to another location.

- Since the origin of the caste system some 3000 years ago, the Dalits have lived in bondage to the Hindu code. There are approximately 300 million people who are deemed "untouchable." In 2001, they rose up to declare their freedom from the system. But what "religion" would guarantee this freedom? Organizations like Gospel for Asia, YWAM and OM rallied to the cause. Through education—Christian education—hundreds of thousands are being touched with the Gospel. Classes of Christian men and women (no longer 'crushed') are graduating and entering the mainstream of Indian life. (www.gfa.org/dalit; www.ywam. org; www.om.org)

"Order your free copy of No Longer A Slumdog."

- Many short-term missions efforts are being integrated carefully into long-term strategies on the field. For example, a missionary in a restrictive country had tried without success for five years to meet the leaders of his target city. When he hosted for just one week a team of professionals from his home country, the leaders of the city openly welcomed them. As the missionary followed up on the group's contact, he exclaimed, "This team opened more doors in one week than I had opened in five years!"

- Mission organizations are accepting more "imperfect" laborers. Many are finding it easier to break through the cultural and personal barriers of the people among whom they minister because they have "been there." Thus, a single American mother is effectively ministering to single moms in Indonesia. A recovered alcoholic is a missionary to alcoholics in Russia. An ex-prostitute is leading women out of the "trade" and into a productive life for the Lord. A blind man is serving well as the Field Personnel Director for an agency. God is releasing non-traditional workers into His harvest!

- The harvest field isn't primarily rural anymore. Over 50% of the world's population now lives in cities. Disenchanted in their search for the "good life" the city was to bring, many are open to the good life in Christ.

- The world is teeming with displaced people. Escaping war, famine, natural disaster or persecution, they are more open to the Gospel than when they lived in their homelands.

- One of the most strategic global outreach efforts is found in the internationals who live among us. It has become a mission field of gigantic proportion. International Students, Incorporated (ISI) has introduced thousands of university students to the One who has *broken down the middle wall of separation* (Ephesians 2:14). Opportunities to minister to other nations' potential leadership range from welcoming them at the airport to hosting them in your home. A powerful ministry, indeed! (www.isionline. org)

- International business people, relocated refugees, ethnic enclaves, illegal aliens, and even international visitors are receptive to friendship evangelism. My wife and I were at the beach watching the seals with a friend from England. A Chinese woman approached me, asking me for the name of the big birds perched here and there. I responded, helping her teach that English word to her two children.

My wife was then impressed to talk with her. 'How long have you been here?' 'Almost a month.' 'Where are you from?' 'Beijing.' 'Have you been in an American home?' 'No.' 'Would you like to visit one?' She jumped at the chance! We had a typical American dinner of baked potato and meatloaf, salad and vegetables. We all held hands as I offered a prayer. She had never eaten a baked potato! She devoured hers, and asked if it would be okay for her to eat the half of her son's that he didn't eat! An invitation for our granddaughter to come and stay with her in China was given. Just three extra places at a meal table and seeds of the Gospel were sown. That's all it takes. (Order a series of twelve essays, *Internationals Who Live Among Us*, available at www.eri.org.)

• Technology is being used as never before. The JESUS Film, a drama portraying the events of the Gospel of Luke, has been viewed by more than 5 billion people in 1114 languages. Through this film alone, it is reported, millions have come to faith in Christ! (www.jesusfilm.org)

• A man whose heart is for the Triqui people in Mexico, puts Christian music and Scripture on "throw-away" SanDisk micro chips. He distributes them as follow up to his ministry among these farm workers.

• Bible studies are being shipped or carried into access-restricted countries on Mp3 players. Airwaves are carrying untold millions of Gospel messages via email and the Internet. Mass media blankets huge population areas. Communication technology has truly connected the world into a global village!

And we see only the tip of the iceberg of our Heavenly Father's business these days. His perspective is infinitely deeper and broader. Beyond human technology, God is showing Himself real to people through dreams and visions. Stories proliferate of Muslims coming to Christ through dreams. (www.answering-islam.org/testimonies)

To better understand and find our part as senders in this awesome task of world evangelization, we must continue to look at the bigger picture of God's purpose on earth in terms of bridging cultural distinctives and establishing strong, evangelizing churches where *"Christ has not yet been preached"* (Romans 15:20). We must ask, "What is the remaining task? What is the status of the Great Commission in today's world?"

> "Muslims are coming to Christ through dreams and visions."

THE WORLD FOR WHOM CHRIST DIED

"You are worthy to take the scroll and to open its seals, because You were slain, and with Your blood You purchased men for God from every tribe and language and people and nation (ethné)."
Revelation 5:9

Missiologists have researched and determined approximately 24,000 people groups in the world. Some of these nations and languages and peoples have heard the Gospel. Some haven't. There are about 16,000 people groups who have embraced the Gospel, resulting in strong churches led by national (non-missionary) leaders with a serious commitment to finish evangelizing the rest of their people. Somewhat over half of the world's population lives in these people groups (ethné). This does not mean all these individuals are Christians; it simply means they live in people groups where it's possible for them to respond to a clear presentation of the Gospel from within their own culture in their own language. But it does point to some good news.

With media focusing on the negative and the evil of the world, it is refreshing to look at these statistics:

It is estimated that by the year 100 A.D., there was only one believer among every 360 people. By 1000 A.D. the ratio had been reduced to 1:270; by 1500, 1:85; by 1900, 1:21; 1970, 1:13. And in the year 2010, there was one Bible-believing, Christ honoring Christian among every 7.3 people. That is good news, indeed!

However, the other half of our planet's residents live in about 8,000 "unreached" people groups. This does not mean that there are no Christians living in these areas. It does mean that there is not a viable, Bible-believing, reproducing church.

While some of these unreached groups are scattered among various world cultures, the majority of them are in five major cultural blocs: 3,300 Muslim people groups; 1200 tribal groups; 2,400 Hindu groups; 100 non-religious groups; and 700 Buddhist groups.

These unreached groups are primarily located geographically in what has come to be called "The 10/40 Window"—from West Africa across Asia between the latitudes of ten degrees north and forty degrees north.

Within this 10/40 window are:

- Most of the world's unreached peoples;

- Two-thirds of the world's population, although it is only one-third of the earth's land area;

- The heart of Islam, Hinduism and Buddhism;

- Eight out of ten of the poorest of the world's poor, enduring the world's lowest quality of living.

Mission statesman Luis Bush, who called Christendom's attention to this region, also points out that the 10/40 Window "is a stronghold of satan."

CHILDREN IN CRISIS

"Let the little children come to Me, and do not hinder them, because the Kingdom of God belongs to such as these."
Mark 10:14

The spiritual need staring at us from the 10/40 Window is staggering. Yet, more recently, Luis Bush has brought another "window" into sharp focus: The "4/14 Window."

The 4/14 Window, first introduced in 1996 by Dan Brewster, refers to the world of children between the ages of four and fourteen years old. Dr Bryant Myers' research showed that 85% of those who become Christians do so between the ages of four and fourteen. Children and teenagers make up half of the world's population. They are vulnerable, impressionable, receptive to what this world is all about. 70% of these children live in the 10/40 Window.

- One-third of the world's population is under the age of 15. This is approximately 2.3 billion children. Every week 2,684,934 more children are born into this world. (That's 140,000,000 a year. Over *one billion, four hundred million* in a ten-year period!) And the numbers grow exponentially. These numbers are difficult to comprehend. Where are these children?

- Two hundred fifty million of these children are working to provide survival-level income for their families.

- One hundred thirty-four million have no access to education.

- One hundred sixty-three million children in our world are orphans. Some of the fortunate ones are in an orphanage. (www.missionfinder.org/orphanages.htm) There are organizations working with orphanages to reunite children with their families. (www.rockministries.org; www.orphancareresources.org)

- One Cairo newspaper declares that Egypt's street kids are victims, not criminals. Between 600,000 and a million children and youth fend for themselves on Cairo streets alone. About 86% of street children have identified violence as a major problem in their life, while 50% stated that they had been exposed to sexual molestation or rape.

- Not limited to Egypt, child exploitation for sex, labor, or house slaves is endemic the world over. In Bangkok, Thailand, a city carrying the inglorious title of "child sex capital of the world," thousands of children are "bought" from hill country families with the promise of educating and training them for good positions, only to be sold to wicked and evil people with the sole purpose of exploiting them. Next to drug trafficking, the sex trade has the highest financial stakes in the world.

- "Throw-away" kids roam the streets, looking for something to eat, keeping a sharp eye out for a safe place to sleep— tonight. They are abused, neglected, exposed to criminal and gang activity, suffer poor health due to their lifestyles and exposure to harsh environments, drug and substance abuse and to STDs.

- Village children walk miles to the city each evening, sleeping in a train station or Christian shelter to avoid being kidnapped and sold into slavery. One gentleman wrote: "We met the slave traders in the open countryside. We negotiated a price with them. We were able to buy most of the children back."

- But what of the generation of children who have the "good life?" The "connected generation" being influenced by the Internet, through Facebook, Twitter, YouTube and scores of other social networking sites? Children who spend their time digitally manipulating characters on the screen whose purpose is to kill and destroy? In 2011, the most popular online game in the world was World of WarCraft. In addition, every day, the children of the world watch 200,000,000 YouTube videos. The connected generation connects, thinks and acts—differently. The Internet is discipling the youth of the world. (www.4to14window. com)

These children are this world's future. The decade represented by the 4/14 Window is the most critical period in terms of human development. During these years, the perspectives of children are profoundly shaped—either positively or negatively. What one generation allows, the next generation embraces.

GOD IS AT WORK THROUGH HIS FAITHFUL FOLLOWERS

"Pray to the Lord of the Harvest, that He will send forth laborers into His Harvest."
Matthew 9:38

As in New Testament times, today there are "Pauls" and "Timothys." Though fewer in number, there are those who follow Paul's example of "going where Christ is not named." They have set bold, adventurous, aggressive goals to penetrate the final frontiers. "I have fully preached the Gospel in these parts ...; I'm going to Spain"—which, in Paul's day, was the end of the earth (Romans 15)!

These 21st-century, forward-thinking missionaries are taking the Mark 16 aspect of the Great Commission: Go! Preach! to every person who has not heard the Good News in a culturally relevant context.

On the other hand, there is a second army of cross-cultural workers whose giftings lead them to follow the Matthew 28 command of the Great Commission: *Go! Teach!* Where daring evangelists of previous generations preached the Gospel of Peace there are today literally thousands of new "Macedonians" standing on the shores of their nations calling, "Come over and help us. Teach us the Word in such a way that we can teach others" (Acts 16:9 and 2 Timothy 2:2). It was Timothy, Titus, Erastus and others that Paul sent to "set in order the things that need attention and appoint elders in every city" (Titus 1:5).

The answer today is two-fold:

1) To identify, challenge and mobilize bold, Pauline-thinking, world-class teams to go directly to the unreached groups of the world, and

2) To increase the number of "Timothys" who will train Two-Thirds World nationals. They will then go to unreached people groups who are more open to them than to Westerners.

Whether your friend is a "Paul" or a "Timothy", whether he joins a pioneer church-planting team, reaches out to the

Christian leaders of the Two-Thirds World or works with children in crisis in Thailand, he needs a strong, as-enthusiastic-as-he-is team of senders—partners in the Gospel, as Paul called the Christians in Philippi.

God will accomplish His historic purpose to "make disciples of all the nations"—the people groups of the world (Matthew 28:19). At the end of time Christ will be exalted with the song: "By Your blood You have purchased for God men from every tribe and tongue and people and nation" (Revelation 5:9). No man knows the day or hour of that fulfillment, but we live in exciting times of opportunity.

> "The world of missions needs bold evangelists and solid Bible teachers."

Today there are nearly two billion worldwide who claim to follow Jesus Christ. Out of these, about 800,000,000 are committed, true believers. Clustered into congregations of about 80—the average size of the world's local church—it's obvious that the Body of Christ now has millions of congregations to impact their own cultures, reach the unreached and serve churches in other cultures.

If some will go. *If* some will serve as senders.

(Many statistics and opportunities for involvement have been shared in this section. Because of God's fast-paced thrust in this 21st century, "numbers" are quickly outdated. For current information about these unreached peoples, the countries they live in and the global efforts to bring the Gospel to them, and other exciting advances in the world of missions, go to the Internet. Look at the websites I have given. Do a simple Google search in any of the areas we have discussed. It will offer all the information for prayer and consideration you need.)

FULL CIRCLE

The Great Commission will be fulfilled. Jesus Christ will offer the blessing of redemption to every nation. From every people group there will be those discipled in Christ's commandments. And to accomplish His historic purpose, God will use a huge harvest force of goers and senders. As Mordecai said to Esther, "Who knows but that you have been brought to the kingdom for such a time as this" (Esther 4:14)? Thus, we also have the privilege to participate in this hour of opportunity.

This challenging scenario—participating in His Great Plan of the Ages—brings us full circle back to you. You are as excited about "a church for every people" as any mission strategist who theorizes that it can be done. You are as zealous for a thriving reproducing church in your adopted people group as the most ardent frontier missionary. You are as passionate as the most effective fulltime evangelist about seeing the lost from every tongue and tribe find new life in Christ. You are as diligent to see God's people discipled in Christian living as any teacher of the Word. But your zeal and passion have been tempered with the knowledge from God that, at least for now, you are to stay right where you are, actively functioning in your local fellowship.

In this chapter we have focused much of our attention on the critical strategy of reaching the unreached. Let's superimpose this plan of "going where the Gospel has not been preached" over the grid of the six sending responsibilities of a support team. What additional opportunities for your involvement will this thrust provide for you?

Moral Support:

Learn all you can about unreached people groups—whether the 10/40 or 4/14 Window. Keep abreast of what is being done to develop and deploy the teams needed. When you hear of a person interested in going to the mission field, encourage him to focus on one of the two thrusts of cross-cultural ministry: training Two-Thirds World nationals to reach the unreached (a "Timothy") or taking the bold drive to "Spain"—to the ends of the earth, with "Paul"!

Read Joshua 1. Listen to God's continual encouragement to

Joshua to *"be strong and of a good courage"* (v. 6). Again, *"Be strong and very courageous..."* (v. 7). Yet again, *"Be strong and of a good courage; be not afraid, neither be discouraged..."* (v. 9). And then, as the people followed God's example (v. 18), you shout the encouragement, *"Be strong and of a good courage!"* This is moral support at its best!

Logistics Support:

If you hold some position (formal or informal) to influence the decision-makers of your church, encourage them to establish corporate mission policies that reflect the two-pronged thrust for training Two-Thirds World nationals and frontier-focused teams. This can be done most directly through the kinds of cross-cultural workers and types of missions with which your church will partner.

When missionary candidates come before your leadership seeking support, discern whether they are part of either a Pauline church-planting team ministry to an unreached people or a Timothy, teaching the Word to national leadership so they may go out to teach others or develop their church as a sending center. Better yet, look among your Body for the cross-cultural "parts" and mobilize them to become part of reaching the unreached.

Prominently display literature and posters that encourage reaching the unreached. Focus on the children. On your church's map of the world, trace the 10/40 Window. Highlight any missionaries you have working in that area or that are training Two-Thirds World nationals to go to that area. Place a small mirror in one of the oceans. Caption it with, "Where in the world do *I* belong?"

Financial Support:

Until you have a specific friend moving into this type of cross-cultural ministry that you can financially support, consider directing your missionary offerings to organizations that are focusing on this massive plan of reaching the unreached. You can begin putting into practice the principles of "living more with less." You can submit yourself to the discipline of wartime austerity. You can encourage others to join you. These ideas can work on both a personal and church level.

Prayer Support:

Stretch your intercession to include this awesome task; prayerfully adopt an unreached people group. Learn about the people. Understand their lifestyle. Become aware of their religious practices. Pray knowledgeably for them. Gather a group around you for corporate prayer for the people, for the organization that will target the group, for the specific team that will enter that group and for the churches that will mobilize, send and support the whole team.

Pray for the mission leaders who are challenging the Body of Christ worldwide to participate in this task of world evangelization. Pray for the several thousand organizations that already have a program focused on the unreached.

> **"Serving as a sender is a challenging and demanding privilege."**

Learn more about praying for unreached people groups through *Operation World*, *Operation China* and the *Global Prayer Digest*. These, and possibly your denomination's prayer guide, will help you focus your prayers on the unreached. (www.missionbooks.org)

Spend an evening at your local library or browse the Internet (or find a teenager who can surf the 'Net' for you) to look up information on the people group your missionary is working among—not just the political country he is in. Jot down findings that are significant to that group's needs, spiritual bondage and possible openings to the Gospel. If the group is one that is already reached and your missionary is equipping them for growth, find out how you can pray that they will become a strong sending center for their own missionaries!

Pray for your church to act more aggressively upon the challenge of reaching the unreached.

Communication Support:

If you do not know any missionaries, contact your denomination's missions division or any one of the mission agencies referred to in this chapter. Express your desire to develop a supporting relationship with someone in a ministry in the area of the world (or people group) or type of ministry (evangelism, Bible translation, etc.) that the Lord has placed on your heart.

Don't forget the children. Develop an email/Skype relationship with the children of missionaries who are living and ministering among the peoples of the world.

Reentry Support:

Review our last chapter and remind yourself of the critical needs of missionaries returning from other cultures. Remember that this area of care is the least talked about and thus the most easily ignored, yet it is one of the most critical. Unreached ethnic groups are especially different from Western culture, so reentry stress is likely to be accentuated in these frontier mission workers. Be an active listener as they process all they experienced.

The experience they've gained and the unique information they've learned is particularly important for the home church—for intelligent prayer and strategic planning. Welcome these returning workers into your home and your life. Let them share what they have been learning—in your home group or at your church. Get them on a radio or TV talk show. Have their story written up in your local secular or Christian newspaper. Have them share at the schools and civic organizations. Give them that opportunity for debriefing their personal issues as well as spreading the news of what God is doing in these awesome hours of history!

(In addition to the individual study below, see the **Group Leader's Guide** for Chapter Eight beginning on page 213.)

FOR YOUR PERSONAL INVOLVEMENT

- Read the story of Esther—it's just a short book. Pay particular attention to Mordecai's challenge to her when she was hesitant about going in to the king (Esther 4:13-14). As history records, Esther fit into God's plan and purpose for her. She truly was called to the kingdom for such a time as that. Throughout the Word, men and women fulfilled His will for their lives and found their place in God's Hall of Faith (Hebrews 11). Mordecai's question, reverberating down through the corridors of time, heard clearly by some generations, ignored by others, is sounding a challenge to you today—a challenge to recognize that you have been called to the Kingdom for a time such as this! It is time to give serious, prayerful consideration: Has God placed a call on your life to serve as a sender?

- Reaching the unreached is such a fast-paced move of God that it is making yesterday's headlines look like ancient history. Because of this, contact some of the organizations whose websites have been listed above to get current information on global breakthroughs among unreached peoples. Be prepared to share those highlights with your fellowship group. If not already, become "Internet-literate" for up-to-date information.

ACTION STEPS

This is it! A decision for personal involvement cannot be put off any longer! By the time you have read Chapter Eight, completed the *For Your Personal Involvement* section and participated in a discussion group, you should ...

- Be able to decide if serving as a sender is the part of the Body of Christ that God has divinely established for you for right now. You might remember that in the very beginning we did say that if not serving as a sender is what God shows you by having read and studied this book, that is a good decision. Move on now to find and actively involve yourself in those "good deeds that He beforehand has determined for you to walk in, for you are His most finely crafted work of art created in Christ Jesus" for that purpose (Ephesians 2:10).

- If you do sense God's calling on your life to serve as a sender but still have not decided on one or another of the six sending responsibilities—or if you would like to do everything, go back over the *For Your Personal Involvement* sections to review each chapter. Find someone who knows you well with whom you can talk, particularly about the giftings and abilities that seem to be the qualifications for each category. Be sure it will be someone who will give you an honest appraisal of your possession of those giftings and abilities!

- If you have heard His confirmation and have found the one or more areas in which to serve as a sender, actively, aggressively pursue and develop this calling. Begin with the ideas given in this book, but don't be limited by them. Be creative. Expand your capacity to serve. Allow His genius to surge through you for, after all, "we have the mind of Christ" (1 Corinthians 2:16).

- Go back to the *For Your Personal Involvement* section of Chapter One, on page 20. If, when you were considering that chapter, you were not able to fill in the statement of the vitality of serving as a sender, reread those Scriptures and prayerfully complete it now.

- Multiply yourself. Having a clear purpose in your own heart and mind, actively seek others in your fellowship who will bind themselves with you in the task of serving as senders. Look for vibrant Christians who have not found their place of ministry yet. It is quite possible they are looking for an opportunity like this. Share the six sending responsibilities with them.

For,

"Whoever will call on the Name of the Lord will be saved. But how will they call on Him if they have not believed in Him? And how can they believe if they have never heard? And how will they hear without someone to tell them? And how can anyone be effective in spreading the Gospel unless he is sent?"

Romans 10:13-15

Epilogue

"I rejoice greatly..."
Philippians 1:5

"I REJOICE GREATLY!" In other words, I am *really* happy! When do we say that? After a good meal? Sitting in the comfort of our home? Relating with people excited about God's Kingdom work? Having a clear picture of His will for our lives? Having just received an "A" in our Greek New Testament language class? At such times, it is easy to rejoice! But, what if you were in prison? Your death sentence has been reprieved once; you are now about to face the Emperor a second time. Could you say with equal enthusiasm, *"I rejoice greatly!"*

Two thousand years ago, a missionary statesman of the First Century was in that prison situation. Yet he said, *"I rejoice greatly!"* What would make a person in that situation say those words? He had been in prison for many years as the result of his false arrest in Jerusalem. How many times did he think about why he had appealed to Caesar? "The Jews made me do it," he once told the leaders in Rome (Acts 28:19).

But here he is, rejoicing greatly. Why? He answers that question: *I rejoice greatly every time I think of you in my prayers, for it brings back to my remembrance how you have been **partners with me in the Gospel** from the very first day even until now* (Philippians 1:4-5).

191

In Acts 16:11, Paul was on his second missionary journey. The Antioch church had commissioned Paul and Silas for this mission. At Lystra, they had picked up Timothy. They were encouraging churches as they went through the regions of Phrygia and Galatia. They were planning to go west into Asia, but the Holy Spirit wouldn't let them. So, they went north to Mysia, intending to go further north into Bithynia. Once again, the Holy Spirit said "No." Not deterred from moving forward, expecting to hear direction from God, they went on to Troas. Paul had a vision of a man from Macedonia: "Come over and help us." Paul picked up Dr. Luke at this point. "Macedonia—Here we come!"

As they crossed over on the Sea of Marmara, they came to the first major Roman city, Philippi. It was a city without ten adult male Jews, so there was no synagogue. Paul and his team met the worshipers by the riverside. Lydia (a merchant woman) and her family were the first to trust in Christ there. That was the very beginning of the church in Philippi that Paul is remembering so many years later.

Now in prison in Rome, he writes a letter of thanks to them for their continuing support.

Moral Support: (Philippians 1:4-5) In this brief Letter, Paul uses words of rejoicing fifteen times. Obviously, his morale is high. I suspect that his morale was high also because he knew of their care in the other five areas.

Prayer Support: (Philippians 1:19 and 14-18) The first area of care Paul addresses is the most critical of all. He says, *"I know this will work out for the good of my soul because of your prayers and the spirit of Jesus Christ."* He has confidence in their prayers for him. But, what is he saying will work out? He has just told them an issue that is bothering him. He is in prison. He cannot preach the Gospel freely. Elsewhere, he said, *"Woe is me if I don't preach the Gospel"* (I Corinthians 9:16). Some of his friends are out there, boldly preaching the Gospel to be an encouragement to Paul. "You can't, Paul, but we will preach to the glory of God." But there are others out there, preaching the Gospel to make Paul feel bad because he can't! "Ha! Ha! Paul, you can't, but we can!" Oh, that must have hurt! He gives the "right" answer: *"Praise God, the Gospel is being preached."* But then he acknowledges that this is an issue still troubling him by his words, "I know this *will* work out...." (How easily we can sometimes give the right answer, yet know that the issue is still bothering us.) But he is confident in the team of prayer warriors in Philippi who are praying for him. And his confidence is also in the spirit of Jesus Christ.

Reentry Support: (Philippians 1:26) *"So you can look forward to great rejoicing when I come to you again, but any boasting will be to the glory of Christ."* I am sure that everywhere that Paul went there was a lot of rejoicing. He had some pretty wild stories to tell, as there will be every time a missionary returns to your church. As Paul enjoined the Christians at Philippi, you want to make sure that all of the rejoicing will be to the glory of God.

You remember what Jesus had to say to His "team" of men when they came back excited about their accomplishments. *"Even the demons were subject to us,"* they boasted. Jesus said, *"Rejoice not that demons are subject to you. Rejoice rather that your names are written in the Book of Life"* (Luke 10:20). Yes, we need to listen to our missionary friends. They need to debrief. They need to process all that they have done and experienced. They need to rehearse the good and the not-so-good, to keep their ministry experience in perspective. Otherwise, if they only talk about the "great and glorious" stories, they can become so enamored with their ministry location that they begin to look negatively at their home culture. Or, only remembering the not-so-good, they could turn their back on missionary work. To focus on either would not be healthy. So, we need to help them in this process. We must also help them with a reality check: Our boasting is in the work of Christ, Who purchased for us eternal Salvation. Our names are in the Book of Life.

Note also in Chapter 2, v28-29, Paul admonishes them on how to receive Epaphroditus when he returns: *"Receive him therefore in the Lord with all gladness, and hold such men in esteem.*" Enough cannot be spoken to encourage the importance of developing a strong, knowledgeable reentry support team!

Logistics Support: (**Phil**ippians **2:25**) Without a modern day currier service, Paul is debating about who should carry this Letter to Philippi. At first, he thought to send it with Timothy. Then he decides to keep Timothy with him *"until I find out how things will go for me here."* So, Paul decides to send Epaphroditus, *"...since he was longing for you, and was distressed because you had heard that he was sick."*

Communication Support: (Philippians 2:25) There is no higher level of communication support than to send one of your fellowship to minister to your missionary. And Paul commends them for sending Epaphroditus, *"...my brother, fellow worker, and fellow soldier, but your messenger and the one who ministered to my needs."*

Financial Support: (Philippians 4:10-19) Dear reader, if the Church around the world could "wrap its collective brain" around the words of Paul's commendation to the people of Philippi regarding money, the whole issue of "missions and finance" would be resolved! He covers the attitude of both the missionary and those who have contributed financially. *"I know how to live well and I know how to be naked and hungry. I have learned how to be content with whatever I have."* Paul was not advocating a "vow of poverty" for missionaries, but a contentment with what the Lord provides through His people.

He continues to express his appreciation that they have been financially supporting him, even when other churches haven't (Philippians 4:14-15). Then he turns his focus from himself to them and what they can expect for their generous giving. *"I don't say this because I wanted a gift from you, but my focus is on the reward you will receive for your kindness."*

In v.18, he brings God into the picture: This financial gift *"is a sweet-smelling aroma, an acceptable sacrifice, well pleasing to God."* Oh, that we, the people of God, would take these words and the words of Jesus to lay up treasures in Heaven (Matthew 6:19-20). That we who give financially would realize that as our missionary friend is giving his life to the work of the Lord, we are giving of our resources to the work of the Lord. Yes, the missionary will be a good steward of those funds, but (with our correct attitude) God is placing that gift to our account on His eternal ledger.

Then, with v.19 (keeping it in this correct context), Paul is saying something like this: You have just given this sacrificial gift to missions, *"But my God shall supply all your needs according to His riches in glory by Christ Jesus."* With the word "but", Paul is tying this thought of God's faithful provision to the previous thought of their sacrificial gift to missions.

Paul concludes, *"The grace of our Lord Jesus Christ be with you all. Amen."*

We rejoice with every testimony we receive telling about missionaries receiving better care. Let us hear your story. Or, if "things aren't working out so well," we would also like to hear from you, too. Maybe we can help!

Neal and Yvonne Pirolo
7150 Tanner Court
San Diego, CA 92111 USA
Phone/Fax: 858-292-7020
Email: Emmaus_Road@eri.org
Website: www.eri.org

Group Leader's Guide

CHAPTER ONE: THE NEED FOR SENDERS

After prayer, summarize the chapter:

❑ From Beth's story, what obviously was wrong?

- Neither she nor her pastor were aware of the critical issue of coming back home.

- Beth was not given (nor took) any opportunity to "debrief"—to verbalize the depth of her experiences.

- Beth may have had an overestimation of her role in missions involvement.

- Her friends didn't detect the symptoms of the trauma she was experiencing.

❑ Paul was a missionary statesman par excellence. Everything we do today to support our missionaries should find its foundation in Scripture.

❑ From Romans 10:13-15, it is clearly established that those who serve as senders share an equal responsibility and privilege with those who go.

❑ Psalm 139:14 says it succinctly: "I am fearfully and wonderfully made." The integrated, yet extremely complex personality of your cross-cultural worker will be stripped of every "comfort zone" he has come to appreciate as he grapples with the various stages of his ministry experience. Because of this, he needs an active, knowledgeable and committed support team working with him while he is preparing to go, while he is on the field and when he returns home.

❑ Each area of support has its unique responsibilities and is best served by specific giftings within the Body of Christ.

❑ Lessons from Byron's story:

- He had a gentle but firm missions pastor and a church with a clear missions statement of how to send missionaries.

- Because of the church leadership's strong support, he could enthusiastically develop his partnership team.

- He initially focused on securing a dedicated core leadership team.

- He made sure that those who joined his team did so because the Lord wanted them to.

- By Anne's question, Byron had obviously built into them a strong sense of ownership of this mission.

Go over the *For Your Personal Involvement section:*

❑ Help the group see the progression of Paul's linear logic establishing the senders as foundational to the goal of the salvation of the lost! It is true that the further one is away from the actual "action" of one praying the "sinner's prayer," the more difficult it is to feel a part of it. Perhaps a couple's experience at being far from the front lines could help illustrate:

We served for a time with Wycliffe Bible Translators in the jungles of Peru. My wife was assigned to keep inventory of the radio parts. For her, a fulltime "people-person," this took some discipline! By tracing the sequence from radio parts to the actual goal of Wycliffe, we were more able to rejoice in such a task. Somebody had to keep up the inventory of radio parts so the radio men could keep the airplane radios in repair so the pilots could fly the linguists to the villages so the linguists could translate the Bible so the indigenous people could have a culturally relevant presentation of the Gospel of Christ so they could put their trust in Him and be saved!

❑ Make sure the nine stages and the incidents in time that mark the transition from one to another are clearly understood.

❑ Read the six passages of Scripture that parallel the six support responsibilities. Make sure everyone sees the application of the Scripture.

❑ Discuss the value of specific giftings for the specific areas of support.

❑ To help crush the ranking of worth made by "cultural Christianity," share Christ's teachings on greatness in the Kingdom of God. Study Mark 10:35-45 and Matthew 18:1-4.

Pray for those who have committed themselves to a study of this book. Ask the Lord for clear insight to which area of support each should become committed. Or, if specific cross-cultural support is not their function in the Body of Christ, pray that that will be equally clear.

For Further Action

❑ Given the structure of your church, how can you proceed to elevate the vitality of the ministry of serving as senders?

❑ Do the missionaries your fellowship or you personally support know of these six areas of care available to them? You might want to survey your missionaries. Have them place the six support ministries in priority. Further, have them rate on some scale from "excellent" to "poor" how adequate they think their support is in each area. Careful! If they are honest with you, what they say may hurt!

❑ From their report, determine clear, deliberate steps to take to bolster the areas of care they sense are lacking.

Chapter Two, Moral Support

After prayer, summarize the chapter:

❑ From Scott and Jean's story:
- God is not the author of confusion, so obviously someone "heard" wrong.
- Commitment as senders is mandatory.
- Support from more than one fellowship is vital.

❑ From the Biblical accounts:
- We see how common to man is the lack of moral support.
- It will take the wisdom of God and conscious effort to reverse the trend.

❑ From the foundation stones:
- Jesus is our example in Word and deed as the Chief Cornerstone.
- Do it simply—and simply do it!
- Moral support is a two-way street.
- Active listening is vital to moral support.
- Commissioning—the call confirmed, the strategy determined and the "laying on of hands"—is vital for the missionaries and for those who serve as senders.

❑ From building awareness:
- There are plenty of resources to encourage and challenge toward moral support.

❑ From Mike's church
- As good as this book is, don't read it while driving!
- We need to break out of the habit, "We've always done it this way!"
- "Home grown" missionaries can more easily develop teams from within the church.

Go over the *For Your Personal Involvement* section:

❑ Have several share their meditations on various translations of Matthew 12:20.

❑ Have a "teaser-length" (1-2 minute) book review of one or more of the books listed or others that have been read.

❑ Identify the kinds of people who can give solid moral support.

❑ Have several read their rewritten story.

❑ Discuss some of this world's philosophies— whether by bumper sticker, commercial jingles or other sources of input— that can distract us from giving moral support.

Pray for those who have made the commitment to actively encourage the Body of Christ. Pray for those who are still uncertain of their place in ministry.

For Further Action

❑ Contrast Joseph's initial response in Matthew 1:18-19 with Elizabeth's first words to Mary on her visit (Luke 1:39-45).

❑ Role play various non-supportive, then supportive responses to the following situations: A person is telling his parents that he thinks God wants him to go on a two-year missionary journey.

❑ Role play: A person is telling his best friend that his parents are angry that he senses God wants him to go on a two-year mission venture.

❑ Role play: An assistant pastor is telling his pastor that a mission agency has invited him to go on a two-year mission venture.

❑ Design your own role play to focus on how to give good moral support!

CHAPTER THREE: LOGISTICS SUPPORT

After prayer, summarize the chapter:

❑ From the story you can emphasize that nobody can do everything. But as everybody does something the job can get done!

❑ Both the Bible and growing mission agency practices are placing the responsibility of initiating the missions process on the local church.

- Identify the cross-cultural parts of your fellowship.

- Give them opportunity to exercise their gifts by being involved in a missions fellowship, by working with internationals in your hometown and by going on a mini-mission.

- Check the accountability of the ministry with which they will work.

- Confirm their spiritual maturity and growth before they go, while they are gone, and when they come home.

- Establish good business practices governing all aspects of your missionary's affairs. If your missionary is going through a mission agency, you as his sending church still need to be aware of their policies, if they actually do what their literature says, and where you fit in.

❑ There are innumerable details that can be handled by a group of individuals.

- How should their material goods be handled?

- Are there family matters to be taken care of?

- What ministry needs can be met?

❑ The Body of Christ needs to care for its members showing diligence, concern for details, punctuality and sound business practices.

❑ From Ray and Susan's story

- A passion for your calling provides strong motivation.

- We *can* bridge the doctrinal distinctives for a common cause.

- Even with the best of plans, things can go wrong.

- The battle rages "behind the lines" as well as at the front.

Go over the *For Your Personal Involvement* section:

❑ Discuss how to overcome the strong individualistic tendencies of our culture. How can we become more involved as the Body of Christ in each other's lives?

❑ Compile a master list from all the logistical needs each person wrote. Don't be overwhelmed! No one person will have all of these needs, but it emphasizes the diversity of needs and the vitality of Logistics Support.

Pray for those who have made a commitment to be a part of the Logistics Support Team for their missionary. Pray for those who have not yet made a commitment to any area of support.

For Further Action

❑ Consider the last missionary your church sent out. Who in the group knows which and to what degree the various logistical needs of that person are being met by your fellowship?

❑ Consider the internationals who live among us. What loss do they sense in not knowing how to establish all the logistics of "setting up" in a new culture? What can you do about it? Order the *All Nations Dictionary*, which is packed with Gospel messages in various definitions, to distribute as gifts to internationals in your area. (Out of print, but Amazon.com has some used copies.) *You Don't Have to Cross the Ocean to Reach the World* by David Boyd is a powerful testimony of local cross-cultural outreach. ERI has a 12 Issue series: *Internationals Who Live Among Us* available at www.eri.org.

CHAPTER FOUR, FINANCIAL SUPPORT

After prayer, summarize the chapter:

❑ From the story you can emphasize God's faithfulness to supply financial support to ministries He directs. When senders diligently seek God for His direction in helping to financially support missionaries, He is faithful to provide the funds— possibly by very unusual methods!

❑ Typical methods of fund-raising do generate some working capital. But for the "long haul," more basic issues of financial management must be tapped:

- Giving. The Biblical principle of tithing yields to cheerful giving, which grows in obedience so "there may be equality." Wise giving carefully chooses who and what to support.

- Lifestyle. Living more with less is an exciting, viable option in comparison to the shallow tenets of the Great American Dream.

- Managing wealth on the field. By carefully supporting economical, effective missionary strategy, you free up money for other decisive cross-cultural work.

- Managing wealth back home. Careful cooperation in any one of the many money-saving and -making enterprises can release finances for missions.

❑ From Sri Lanka and the Middle East

- Even in cultures less familiar with the missions process, progress is being made.

- The principles of *Serving As Senders—Today* are universal, in that they are taken from Scripture.

Go over the *For Your Personal Involvement* section:

❑ From Scripture, discuss the philosophy of financial support Paul the Apostle seems to have adopted.

❑ Tithing is one principle of the Kingdom of God. It works!

❑ Encourage discussion surrounding the five questions on page 81. Avoid condemnation either of yourselves or others; however, allow the Holy Spirit His opportunity to convict in the area of our wealth.

❑ Media input first sells us on our needs, then provides us with the plastic money to mortgage our future. Have someone share a vibrant testimony of victory over credit card buying.

Pray for those who have made a commitment to be a part of a missionary's Financial Support Team and for those who are still uncertain as to their personal involvement in serving as a sender.

For Further Action

❑ Consider sponsoring a Christian financial management seminar.

❑ Do a study on the financial accountability of the organizations with which your missionaries are working. (www. davidmays.org/agency partner.pdf has material to help you ask the right questions. Also, consider purchasing his *Stuff* CD.)

❑ Do a study on the financial accountability of your missionaries.

CHAPTER FIVE, PRAYER SUPPORT

After prayer, summarize the chapter:

❑ From the two opening stories, it is clear that commitment to prayer is not to be lightly regarded; rather, it is a discipline of long-term obedience.

❑ Though the effectiveness of prayer is a divine mystery, the practice of prayer is as clear as any Bible story.

❑ Prayer is the arena of spiritual warfare. Only the well-advised should enter there.

❑ The prayers of the Bible can serve as models for our prayers. These prayers provide for us the language and nature of petitions in line with the heart of God.

❑ Prayer with fasting is a powerful weapon in the spiritual warfare we are facing with our cross-cultural worker.

❑ "In-the-gap" praying is a level of intercession that demands a depth of commitment beyond the novice.

❑ "The harvest is plentiful; the laborers are few" is as true today as when Jesus spoke it. Therefore, "pray to the Lord of the harvest to send forth laborers" (Matthew 9:37-38).

❑ From the church in Sacramento
  • It is more difficult to check on accountability in the area of prayer support.
  • There needs to be good coordination between the communications and prayer leaders.
  • Prayer takes time!

Go over the *For Your Personal Involvement* section:

❑ Discuss the types of prayers the group has been used to praying.

❑ Discuss several model prayers of Jesus and other Bible characters that have been studied, and what differences the group anticipates in their praying now.

❑ Have someone who has prepared ahead of time give a book review of *God's Chosen Fast*.

❑ Have available the contact addresses of your church's missionaries for those who are ready to make a commitment to their prayer support.

Pray for those who have made a commitment to be a part of a cross-cultural worker's Prayer Support Team. Pray for those who have yet to make a commitment to any area of support.

For Further Action

❑ Begin a mission prayer group, or increase awareness of the existing one(s).

❑ Give a more prominent visual place to the prayer requests of your missionaries by

- Posting letters on church bulletin board with prayer requests highlighted.
- Putting excerpts of those requests in the church bulletin each week or month.
- Requesting regular public congregational prayer for specific needs of your missionaries.

❑ Expand the vision of your church's outreach by using a world prayer guide such as the *Global Prayer Digest, Operation China* or *Operation World.*

❑ Prayer support is the most vital of the six areas.

- History tells of many who forged their way to God's chosen fields of the world without Moral Support. But they got there.
- Having one or more friends back home handling all of the Logistics Support eases the mind of the cross-cultural worker. But they have survived without it.
- Financial Support does provide nicely for the worker's needs. But the belt can be tightened.

(And the two yet to be considered.)

- News from a far country provides great Communication Support. But loneliness can be handled.
- Reentry Support certainly shores up the unstable as they come back home. But life goes on.

These five areas of support relate to the physical, emotional and psychological well-being of your missionary friend. Though the adjustments for lack of support in these areas are difficult, they can be made. However, Prayer Support moves into the realm of the spiritual where there is no adjustment for lack of support! Therefore, make this issue the highest priority.

CHAPTER SIX, COMMUNICATION SUPPORT

After prayer, summarize the chapter:

❑ From the Paris missionary's story:
- God is merciful, but there is a better part of wisdom that says missionaries should get some good, practical training.
- Working with nationals enabled her to stay in the country.
- It was fortunate for her to see a positive example.

❑ From Mary's story:
- Even returning missionaries face difficulties that are helped by communication support.
- The encouragement of communication support doesn't always take away the difficulty, but it sure helps your missionary through it.

❑ From the Biblical writers:
- Make the communication real.
- Be personal.
- Even short notes should be written and sent.
- Communication support is for their benefit.
- Don't feel you have to say everything you know.
- Reminders are good.
- Sometimes your communication might be a God-inspired exhortation.

❑ Get *everyone* involved in communicating with your missionaries.

❑ Be sure the content is worth reading.

❑ Use all methods of communication:
- Phone, fax, telex, ham radio, photos, CDs, DVDs, blogs, text messaging, Skype, Facebook, Twitter, care packages, visits ... and the list goes on!

❑ From the story in Spain
- When a denomination brings churches into the missions process, the missionaries need to cooperate.
- Teams were developed well with the Latin American leadership

Go over the *For Your Personal Involvement* section:

❑ Have several share their highlighted Letter of Paul. What was mundane in the Letter—yet important enough to be included in Scripture? What did some of the other writers talk about?

❑ Make a list as the group relates the many different types of communication support your missionaries have received.

❑ What have other churches found to be practical ways toward communication support?

❑ Compile a list of the resources within your group for communication support.

Pray for those who have made the commitment to be a part of a missionary's Communication Support Team. Pray for those who have not yet made a decision regarding any area of support.

For Further Action

❑ Right now, let each one present have a half sheet of paper to write a personal note to your missionary. Scan them into one email attachment and send it—tonight!

❑ Prepare a chart to show what time it is where your missionary is living. Find out from him the best times to reach him by telephone or Skype.

❑ Talk with the Children's Minister or Sunday School superintendent. Develop a plan for the children to communicate with missionary children in other countries.

❑ Set up a touch screen computer in the foyer of your church.

CHAPTER SEVEN, REENTRY SUPPORT

After prayer, summarize the chapter:

❑ From the seminary director's story:
- The devastation of this missionary's "crash" rippled out far beyond the circle of his immediate family.
- No doubt many factors beyond reentry stress contributed to his "spiritual suicide." But if he had had a good Reentry Support Team to unload on, what grief might have been averted!

❑ From the Situation of Reentry:
- Reentry shock is the initial response and deals more with environmental changes your worker must face.
- Reentry stress deals more with the deeper struggles of attitude and spiritual motivation that run contrary in the two cultures.

❑ From the Challenge of Reentry:
- Become very familiar with these nine areas. It is in one or more of these areas that you will sense some struggle in your returning cross-cultural worker.
- Know your worker well. Think beyond the examples given to specific issues that might frustrate him upon reentry.

❑ From the Reentry Behavior Patterns:

- Alienation, condemnation and reversion sometimes provide the degenerative spiral down to the fourth, the ultimate escape—emotional, mental, spiritual or physical suicide. Be aware of these and if you notice the signs, try to divert the returned missionary from this destruction.

- The focus of your reentry program should be on the fifth pattern: Integration!

- Integration is on two levels: The immediate needs of living and long-range interaction.

- The most vital, immediate issue on either level is the need for active listening.

- The Reentry Team must provide opportunities for debriefing. This is as much for your worker's benefit as it is for the edification of the group listening.

- In time, slowly help your worker become involved in some meaningful level of ministry.

- Consider the specific needs of the various family members or of the single adults.

❑ From the story in Washington

- When you see symptoms of something wrong, you don't just do "nothing!"

- Reentry care demands a knowledgeable team.

- The Northwest office, motivated by this death, took good action.

- Any good program needs ongoing care.

Go over the *For Your Personal Involvement* section.

❑ Review any articles on the subject of reentry.

❑ Hear the real stories of reentry given by returned missionaries.

❑ Develop a plan for educating the Body on this area of support.

Pray for those who have made the commitment to be a part of their missionary's Reentry Support Team. Pray for those who have not yet made a decision regarding any area of support.

For Further Action

❑ Purchase *The Reentry Team: Caring For Your Returning Missionaries*. Read and apply!

❑ Obtain information that various international corporations use to bring their employees home. Incorporate transferable material to your program of reentry.

❑ In the opening chapter of this book, we related Beth's story in which she was so distraught by her lack of reentry support that she chose to take her own life. By God's mercy, that plan was thwarted. Unfortunately, there are other less final but critically serious forms of suicide that may require professional help. If it appears that a returning missionary is not responding to the care you are able to provide, there are groups equipped to help.

One organization in the USA is Link Care Center, www.linkcare.org; Info@linkcare.org. Another contact is: Quiet Waters Ministries: www.quietwatersministries.org; jims@qwaters.org.

❑ There may be members of your fellowship who would like to participate in a broader hospitality ministry to missionaries. Makahiki Ministries is dedicated to providing short-term hospitality housing around the world for missionaries. To find out how you can help missionaries find a respite from their hectic pace, contact Makahiki Ministries:www.hospitalityhomes.org; makahiki@zoho.com. Another excellent contact is Life Impact Ministries: www.lifeimpactministries.net; david.grissen@lifeimpactministries.net.

Also, most mission agencies are looking for senders willing

to open their homes in hospitality to returning missionaries. One such agency is Wycliffe Bible Translators: www.wycliffe.org; Info_USA@wycliffe.org.

Chapter Eight, Your Part in the Big Picture

After prayer, summarize the chapter:

❑ Those in the global Christian community are taking bold, aggressive steps to mobilize and deploy thousands of new missionaries to reach the unreached. The growing force is coming from the Two-Thirds World. God is using scores of untraditional methods and people in His Harvest.

❑ Major initiatives, such as NEMA, Back to Jerusalem and CPM are having an impact on world missions.

❑ God is doing a mighty work among the nations. Yet about half of the earth's population lives beyond a simple, culturally relevant presentation of the Gospel.

❑ Most of the world's 8000 unreached people groups—in five major blocks—live in a geographic region called the 10/40 Window.

❑ Until recently, very little has been done to target these people. In fact, today only about 10% of the world's missionary force is working among unreached peoples.

❑ They can be reached by a two-pronged attack:

1) God is sovereignly raising up an army of new Two-Thirds World nationals to go as missionaries to the unreached. Send thousands of "Timothys" to teach them the Word in such a way that they will teach others (2 Timothy 2:2).

2) Identify, mobilize, train and deploy thousands of "Pauline-bold" teams to penetrate these final frontiers of unreached peoples.

❑ The 4/14 Window brings new emphasis to children in crisis.

❑ The Body of Christ worldwide now has the resources to "make disciples of every nation"—of every people group.

❑ As part of this worldwide move, we can actively serve as senders in the six areas of support as they relate to reaching the unreached.

Go over the *For Your Personal Involvement* section:

❑ Focus on that most critical question Mordecai gave to Esther: "Who knows but that for an hour such as this, you have been called to the kingdom?" Relate and discuss other Scriptures that lay a responsibility for action on us to participate in God's Great Commission (Genesis 12:1-3; Isaiah 6:8; John 20:21; Matthew 28:18-20; Mark 16:15; James 1:22).

❑ Have individuals share the information they obtained from the many websites mentioned. Pray as various ones share global breakthroughs on what God is doing to reach every people.

For Further Action

❑ Have a dedication for those who signed the statement in Chapter One. Create your own form to include the area(s) of care to which they have committed. Guard against denigrating those who believe serving as senders is not for them. Encourage them to find their place of ministry within the Body of Christ.

❑ Use this group for the formation of a missions fellowship. Aggressively engage this group in taking their responsibility before God for your church's part in His "big picture."

Resources

FOR FURTHER STUDY

Check with your church, denomination or mission agency for their mission vision resources. It is best to keep your vision in line with the goals of your church.

Following is a list of current (and classic) books highly recommended by the missions community. Many are available as ebooks. It would be well for many of them to be in your church's missions library, and given periodic reviews in Sunday School and church and home gatherings. These books may be available from 1) your local Christian bookstore, 2) the publisher listed, or 3) STL Distribution: 1-8-MORE-BOOKS (1 866 732-6657).

Motivation for Missions

A Mind for Missions, Paul Borthwick (NavPress) Learn how to make God's passionate heart for the world a part of your daily life.

From Jerusalem to Irian Jaya: A Biographical History of Christian Missions, Ruth Tucker (Zondervan) An excellent "thumbnail" history of missions.

Let the Nations be Glad!, John Piper (Baker Books) Worship, the ultimate goal of the church, fuels missions. Missions is, because worship is not.

Perspectives—A Reader, Ralph Winter and Steven Hawthorne–ed. (William Carey Library) Biblical, Historical, Cultural, Strategic perspectives on the World Christian Movement.

The Great Omission—A Biblical Basis for World Evangelism, Robertson McQuilkin (Gabriel Publishing) This Biblically-based investigation answers the question, "Why isn't missions a priority today?"

Strategies for Missions

101 Ways to Change Your World—Personal Evangelism That Really Makes a Difference, Geoff Tunnicliffe (Gabriel Publishing) Practical ways to do missions today—right where you are.

A Guide to Short-Term Missions—A Comprehensive Manual for Planning an Effective Missions Trip, Dr. Leon Greene (Gabriel Publishing) A thorough look at the challenges and blessing facing anyone preparing for a short-term missions trip.

Eternity in Their Hearts, Don Richardson (Regal Books) The concept of an eternal God can be found in hundreds of cultures around the world.

God is at Work, Ken Eldred (Regal) Possibly the best single read on Business as Mission, and transforming people through business.

Marching to a Different Drummer, Jim Raymo (Christian Literature Crusade) Rediscovering missions in an age of affluence and self-interest.

Missions in the 21st Century, Tom Telford (Harold Shaw Publishers) Practical helps for getting your church into the game.

Out of the Saltshaker and into the World, Rebecca Pippert (InterVarsity Press) Let your life be poured out in a way to make the world "thirsty" for God.

Postmission—World Mission By a Postmodern Generation, Editor Richard Tiplady (Authentic Publishing) Addressing significant cultural changes in the West and new ways of 'doing' missions.

Tentmakers Speak, Don Hamilton (TMQ Research) This book considers the advantages and difficulties of modern "tentmaking."

Tentmaking: Business as Mission, Patrick Lai (Authentic) The results of an extensive survey on workable alternatives to conventional missionary life.

The Discovery of Genesis, C.H. Kang and Ethel R. Nelson (Concordia) Hidden in the ancient Chinese characters is the story of the Bible.

The Jesus Style, Gayle D. Erwin (Ronald N. Haynes Publishers) A challenge to incarnate the lifestyle of Jesus in your daily living.

Jesus in Beijing, David Aikman A compelling story of the broad scope and depth of Christianity in China.

*The World at Your Door*step, Lawson Lau (InterVarsity Press) A challenge to minister among internationals who are living among us.

Today's All Star Missions Churches—Strategies to Help Your Church Get in the Game, Tom Telford (Baker) A study of churches which are deeply involved in missions. Great ideas for your church!

Prayer Support

Destined for the Throne, Paul Billheimer (Bethany House Publishers, Christian Literature Crusade) Here is a message of God's love for His Son's Bride. It is a powerful call to prayer.

God's Chosen Fast, Arthur Wallis (Christian Literature Crusade) The classic on why, when, where and how to fast.

Operation China, Paul Hattaway (Piquant) Excellent prayer information for the 490 minority groups of China. Beautiful pictures; accurate information.

Operation World—21st Century Edition, Patrick Johnstone & Jason Mandryk (Authentic Publishing) This book is packed with inspiring information for prayer about every country of the world.

Piercing the Darkness, Frank Piretti (Crossway Books) The influence of the unseen world in the affairs of life are dramatically suggested in this novel, challenging us to prayer.

This Present Darkness, Frank Piretti (Crossway Books) A wild fantasy of the unseen battle between good and evil, challenging us to prayer.

Touch the World Through Prayer, Wesley Duewel (Zondervan) Each chapter will teach you about the power of intercessory prayer.

Windows on the World—When We Pray God Works, Daphne
     Spraggett & Jill Johnstone (Authentic Publishing)
     Stunning photographic visuals illustrate information and
     prayer points for 100 countries and people groups.

Reentry Support
Culture Shock, Myron Loss (Light and Life Press) Learn how
     your missionary needs to deal with the stress of cross-
     cultural living.
Doing Member Care Well, Kelly O'Donnell-ed (William Carey
     Library) A reference book of network, specialist, send and
     self care for missionaries.
Families on the Move, Marion Knell (Monarch Books) Practical
     approaches to preparing for the mission field, building
     bridges with 'home' and making right choices.
Honorably Wounded, Marjory Foyle (Monarch Books) Helps
     for stress among Christian workers.
Raising Resilient MKs, Joyce Bowers – ed. (ACSI) Resources for
     Caregivers, Parents and teachers.
Re-Entry, Peter Jordan (YWAM Publishing) Making the
     transitions from Missions to Life at Home.
The Reentry Team: Caring for Your Returning Missionaries, Neal
     Pirolo (Emmaus Road Intl.) Through 70 case studies, the
     Church learns how to serve in this most neglected area of
     missionary care.
Third Culture Kids, David Pollock and Ruth Van Reken
     (Nicholas Brealey Publishing) A very personal approach to
     transition and change for global nomads.
To Understand Each Other, Paul Tournier (Westminster John
     Knox) How to reverse the trend that most conversations of
     the world are "dialogues of the deaf."
We Really Do Need to Listen, Reuben Welch (Impact Books)
     In his unique style, the author brings to light the greatest
     need in human relationship.

Financial Support
Friend Raising—Building a Missionary Support Team That Lasts,
     Betty Barnett (YWAM Publishing) Vital help for those
     building their support team. An excellent counterpart of
     this book, *Serving As Senders—Today*.

Funding Your Ministry, Scott Morton (Dawson Media)
Excellent Bible studies and practical training.

Getting Sent, Peter Sommer (Intervarsity Press) A relational
approach to support raising.

Living More With Less, Doris Janzen Longacre (Herald Press)
Learn how to enhance your lifestyle while spending less
money.

People Raising, Bill Dillon (Moody Press) Basic support raising
principles.

Inspiring Stories of Missions and Missionaries

A Chance to Die, Elizabeth Elliott (Fleming H Revell) The life
of Amy Carmichael, an Irish missionary.

A Distant Grief, F. Kefa Sempangi (Regal Books) An African
pastor's poignant account of a nation destroyed by a
godless murderer and his false religion.

Bruchko, Bruce Olson (Creation House) The astonishing true
story of a 19-year-old missionary among the Motilone
Indians in South America.

By Their Blood, James & Marti Helfey (Baker Books) A record
of Christian martyrs of the 20th Century.

Chasing the Dragon, Jackie Pullinger (Hodder & Stroughton)
The amazing story of breaking the bondage of opium
addiction in Hong Kong.

Death of a Guru, Rabi R. Maharaj (Harvest House)
Autobiography of a Hindu, destined to become a guru,
who trusted in Christ, instead.

End of the Spear, Steve Saint (SaltRiver) The riveting story of
Steve meeting his father's killer and their life together.

I Dared to Call Him Father, Bilquis Sheikh (Chosen Books) The
riveting story of a Muslim woman to whom Jesus appeared
in a dream.

Lifting the Veil—A World of Muslim Women, Phil & Julie
Parshall (Gabriel Publishing) A heart-wrenching and
perplexing look at the true world of Muslim women.

Lords of the Earth, Don Richardson (Regal Books) The
incredible tale of Irian Jaya's Snow Mountains Yali people
and their encounter with Christ.

Peace Child, Don Richardson (Regal Books) Come to
    understand the concept of "redemptive analogy" through
    the story of Sawi people.
Shadow of the Almighty: The Life and Testament of Jim Elliot,
    Elizabeth Elliot (Harper & Row) A life-challenging
    biography of Jim Elliot.
The Amazing Danis, David Scovill (Xulon Press) How
    thousands of Dani came to Christ in Papua and have an
    enduring church today.
The Heavenly Man, Brother Yun (Monarch books) The
    incredible miracles of a faithful Chinese Christian.
Through Gates of Splendor, Elizabeth Elliot (Living Books) The
    true story of the martyrdom of five men in Equador.
Tortured for His Faith, Haralan Popov (Zondervan) An epic of
    Christian courage under severe persecution.
Unveiled at Last, Bob Sjogren (Crown Ministries, Intl) Exciting
    stories of God's unchanging purpose to redeem some for
    every tribe, tongue, and people.
Vanya, Myrna Grant (Creation House) A true story of ruthless
    persecution in the Red Army and Vanya's courage through
    it.
Youth and Missions, Paul Borthwick (Gabriel Publishing) A
    practical handbook that provides principles, guidelines and
    examples of how to involve youth in missions.

For Updated Search
    Because of the fast-paced culture in which we live and the
rapidly changing landscape of our world and how to reach
people for Christ, visit the Internet! A Google search will put
you in touch with thousands of sites on any conceivable aspect
of world evangelization.

RESOURCES AVAILABLE THROUGH EMMAUS ROAD INTERNATIONAL

ACTS Media Resources
Prepare for Battle!—This 8-hour DVD comes with 19 pages
    of Student Notes and Assignments and a Study Guide for
    Groups or Individuals.

Serving As Senders—This 6-hour DVD is the "book" live!

For Those Who Go—This 5+hour DVD takes a long look at many cross-cultural issues and their solutions.

What's The Big Deal? They're Just Coming Home!—The attitude expressed in the title of this 2-hour DVD is only one of 34 factors that make coming home so difficult for a missionary.

Developing Your Partnership Team—This 2-hour DVD or CD is the counterpart of the book, *Serving as Senders—Today,* instructing the missionary in how to develop relationships in the six areas of support.

Solutions to Culture Stress—This 4-hour DVD helps prepare a short-term missionary for the culture stress of going overseas and returning home.

ACTS Media Library—A Library of various titles for free download. (www.eri.org)

Publications

Critical Issues in Cross-Cultural Ministry are 4-6 page bulletins written on vital missions topics. Reprints available:

Series I: Mobilizing Your Church 15 Issues

Series II: For Those Who Go 15 Issues

Series III: Serving As Senders 12 Issues

Series IV: Internationals Who Live Among Us 12 Issues

Serving As Senders—Today: How to Care for Your Missionaries— While They are Preparing to Go, While They are on the Field, and When They Return Home.

Prepare For Battle: Basic Training in Spiritual Warfare—Making reference to over 700 Scriptures that point to victory in battle, this book drives home the importance of practicing the basics in spiritual warfare.

The Reentry Team: Caring for Your Returning Missionaries—This study book zeros in on the least understood and most difficult time in the life of a missionary, and how you can help.

I Think God Wants Me to be a Missionary: Issues to Deal with Long Before You Say "Good-bye"—Everybody likes a story. This is a story of four young people who make that statement to their pastors. Through dialogue, 25 people get involved in discovering solutions to scores of issues that come up.

Sirviendo al enviar Oberos: Como apoyar a sus misioneros—Serving As Senders in Spanish. For information about publishers of other translations of *Serving As Senders*, visit www.eri.org/publications.

Seminars

Nothing GOOD Just Happens! Seminar—This is an intense, 21-hour seminar to train church missions leadership in how to mobilize their fellowship in cross-cultural outreach ministry.

For Those Who Go Seminar—The sessions of this 6-hour seminar help the potential cross-cultural worker look beyond the "romanticism" of missions and to deal with some very practical issues of going.

Serving as Senders Seminar—The lessons of the book, *Serving as Senders—Today*, are presented in a 6-hour format.

Prepare for Battle!—The lessons of the book by that title are presented in a 6 to 9-hour format.

What's the Big Deal? They're Just Coming Home! Seminar—This two- or three-hour seminar will help train you in caring for your missionary friends at this crucial time of coming home.

Developing Your Partnership Team Seminar—This two- or three-hour seminar will train the missionary in how to develop his partnership team.

ACTS Ministry Trips

ERI leads three-week trips throughout the year. Pre-field training, a demanding "hands-in" experience and follow through after the trip helps the church leadership develop a consistent involvement in missions.

Speakers Bureau

Neal and Yvonne Pirolo, and associates of Emmaus Road are available as speakers on a variety of subjects, all challenging to a personal involvement in cross-cultural outreach ministry.

For more information on these or other developing resources to equip you and your church for cross-cultural ministry, contact us.

Emmaus Road International
7150 Tanner Court • San Diego, CA 92111 USA
858 292-7020 • Emmaus_Road@eri.org • www.eri.org

Notes

Notes

Notes

Notes

Notes

Notes